ANIMALS *Speak*

WHAT ANIMALS WANT YOU TO KNOW: 10 SHORT STORIES

ROMMIE BUHLER

First published in 2022 by Rommie Buhler

© Rommie Buhler

The moral rights of the author have been asserted.
This book is an Inspirational Book Writers book.

Author: Buhler, Rommie

Title: ANIMALS SPEAK; What Animals Want You To Know: 10 Short Stories

ISBN: 9798370480195

All rights reserved. Except as permitted under the Australian Copyright Act 1968 (for example, a fair dealing for the purposes of study, research, criticism, or review), no part of this book may be reproduced, stored in a retrieval system, communicated, or transmitted in any form or by any means without prior written permission. All enquiries should be made to the author at *hello@rommiebuhler.com*

Editor-in-chief: Rachel Koontz
Cover Design: Sarah Rose Graphic Design
Cover image: Canva

Disclaimer:
The material in this publication is of the nature of general professional advice, but it is not intended to provide specific guidance for particular circumstances, and it should not be relied on as the basis for any decision to take action or not take action on any particular matter which it covers. Readers should obtain individual advice from the author where appropriate, before making any such decision. To the maximum extent permitted by law, the author and publisher disclaim all responsibility and liability to any person, arising directly or indirectly from any person taking or not taking action based on the information in this publication.

Legal Disclaimer
Please be advised that no intuitive, animal communication, energy healing, medical intuitive or intuitive investigation work can predict, forecast, diagnose or provide information with absolute certainty. No guarantees or assurances of any kind are given and Rommie Buhler will not be held accountable for any interpretations or decisions made by readers based on information provided in this book. Th e content of this book is written for entertainment and information purposes only and is not meant to replace veterinary or professional care. Please always consult with a veterinarian for medical and health concerns.

TESTIMONIALS

HOLY CRAP!!!!! She Just woke me up, jumped on my bed while I'm in it, hasn't done that since she was a kitten, spent 15-20 minutes demanding pats and drooling on me. Then sat on bed head for a bit and then casually wandered off not running away!!! Started flower essences Saturday and every second day doing exercises. I've been doing the EFT and then the energy grafting through the body you suggested for Taj too, thought it might simulate being patted.

Jamie, Cat, Australia

After just one remote healing session the vet is shocked. Stevie is making progress, I saw the difference in him almost immediately after your healing was sent, the vet was shocked and admitted he expected the opposite result, so much gratitude!

Dog (with Slipped Disc), United Kingdom

OMG, I first heard Rommie on the radio and was inspired to have my then horse read. AMAZING. So accurate and found out things I had no idea about. I have since had full and part readings with my Cat, Dog and new Horse. It has also made me more aware and open to checking in with my animals from time to time to see how they are. Love ya work.

Rowena, Horse, Australia

Cody was acting weird and that's why I contacted Rommie. She tuned in and she suggested Cody being in pain and that pain was coming from his face. I checked his ears, palpated his face and sure enough I found out that he had a broken tooth with a draining cyst which caused the discomfort. I had the tooth extracted and Cody was back to his old self.

Cody, Dog, USA

Rommie contacted my horse to see if there was anything more we can do to help her, I had not given her any information at all and she came back with exactly what the vet had diagnosed. It was good to know things were stable and not deteriorating. Thank you Rommie.

Anonymous, Horse, New Zealand

Incredible. Rommie was able to tune into my Lettie, 9 yo Cavoodle and determine the cause of her medical issue which was quickly resolved. A change in her diet as suggested, has made a huge difference in her energy level and her coat is beautiful and healthy & soft (the rough dry hair that came through and was cut off blew my mind). Her anxiety-barking has significantly reduced by using positive language. I'm so happy.

Marsha, Dog, Australia

I learned so much from my Animal Communication session with Rommie. My cat, Soli, has multiple health issues and I needed the expertise that Rommie shares so generously to understand and save my baby. Rommie shared Soli's precious thoughts and feelings with me and I truly feel closer to my Kitty since our session. Rommie took each of my questions about Soli's health and lovingly communicated them to Soli, helping me understand how I might help to heal what ails her. I have already put some ideas into practice and I'm excited to see what the future holds. Thank you, Rommie, from the bottom of my heart! Have faith and try Animal Communication with Rommie!

Colleen, Cat, USA

Rommie Buhler

Rommie is amazing! She is kind, compassionate, understanding and her incredible intuition during Ruby's reading was spot on. She picked up on the issues Ruby is having, plus more. I feel I have a greater understanding and can confidently follow up on the advice she has given us. The whole experience was enlightening and reaffirming at the same time. I am so grateful to have been directed to Rommie and I know we will speak again!

Kim, Dog, Australia

*I dedicate this book to the animals that continue to
wake me up at 2 a.m. insisting I help them.*

TABLE OF CONTENTS

FOREWORD xi

AUTHOR'S NOTE.. xiii

INTRODUCTION.. xvii

NORMAN HAS ANXIETY AND
A NAME CHANGE 1
[Read this chapter if your animal is suffering from anxiety.]

VELVET ROSE GOES ON A HUNGER STRIKE 13
[Read this chapter if your animal has been having behavioural changes.]

SAM GETS A LESSON FROM
HER BABY TIGERS 23
[Read this chapter if you are having trouble understanding your cats.]

MR. BANKS DETECTS A PROBLEM 33
[Read this chapter if your animal is unusually and extremely anxious.]

CALENDULA SOLVES THE MYSTERY OF KALEENA
GALE'S ODD BEHAVIOUR 45
*[Read this chapter if your horse is throwing its rider,
biting, or balking at jumps.]*

WINNIE'S TICKET TO FREEDOM COMES UNDONE 55
[Read this chapter if your animal has gone missing.]

STOP SCRATCHING, AUGUST! 67
[Read this chapter if your animals are constantly itchy and scratching.]

**SCOTTY HAS AN ADDICTION HE
CAN'T SHAKE** 75
[Read this chapter if your cat has an addiction to kibble and kidney problems.]

THE WORST MORNING OF HARLEY'S LIFE 85
[Read this chapter if your animal is puzzlingly unwell.]

**THE RUSTLERS PUT A HOLE IN MY HEART
AS BIG AS THE GRAND CANYON** 93
[Read this chapter if you have had an animal stolen and not returned.]

33 THING OUR ANIMALS NEED US TO KNOW 101

RESOURCES 167

ACKNOWLEDGMENTS 169

FIND ROMMIE BUHLER ONLINE 171

**ONLINE ANIMAL COMMUNICATION
TRAINING** 173

HOW HAS THIS BOOK HELPED YOU? 177

FOREWORD

I have known Rommie Buhler for 18 years, meeting through mutual friends including her husband Jason, whom we all shared cycling and triathlon as a sporting interest. Rommie is a professional, relatable, energetic and empathetic person, who also connects with animals. She has a strong sense of self, is an honest straight talker, and stands bravely for who she is and what she believes in, even through the challenges of a road less travelled.

Having mutual friends, and a love for the animals in our lives, Rommie and I remained connected over many years, but it was when she transitioned her career path towards intuitive animal communication, that I became somewhat intrigued. As a veterinarian, this would be a useful tool, but beyond the scope of what I understood, and beyond the belief of my education and training. As a veterinarian, it is also easy to 'pigeon hole' people who have such claims.

A valuable lesson I have learned in my profession are the things we most often resent or criticise, are the things we fear or just don't yet understand. As people, we have a choice to remain open minded and attempt to learn more about the things or people we resent or criticise, or continue to do so. The outcome of these learnings may confirm the scepticism was warranted, or even better may confirm there is validity and value for such a skill set or person in our lives or profession, even if we don't fully understand the process.

Rommie has performed several readings on our animals, including her integral input into locating our very much loved missing

Burmese cat, checking in on them following behavioural changes, and the explanation of a relocation. I don't completely comprehend the process, but I don't need to, just as she doesn't need to know how to perform lifesaving surgery on an animal. I do however, highly value the input she has had into the relationship I have with animals in my life. Rommie communicates her readings honestly and responsibly, and recognises that her communications are not meant in anyway to replace health professional advice, but more importantly to open the dialogue of the subject with owners, and help direct the most appropriate collaborative actions.

When Rommie asked me to write the foreword for her book, I was excited that her experiences and knowledge would be shared, but I was also conflicted. How, as a member of the veterinary profession could I endorse a book that challenged the trained scientific logic that we are conditioned to? On reflection, I realised that the two are not mutually exclusive, rather an opportunity for collaboration and integration. An opportunity to endorse the intent of the subject matter, which is aligned with all animal care providers, all of which have an overarching goal that is greater than their own individual professions, and that is: to improve the health and wellbeing of animals, and the connection and relationship they have with the humans in their lives.

So I challenge you to open your mind, pick the book up, and embark on an interesting, sometimes light-hearted, sometimes solemn, but always thought provoking, journey of what animals have to say about their lives and their humans. If everyone who reads this book relates to one short story, or small snippet of information, that leads to an improved outcome for an animal's wellbeing; and if everyone who reads this book finishes it with increased empathy and understanding of the animals around them; then we should all be grateful for the words within. Congratulations Rommie Buhler.

Rachael Smith
Veterinarian

AUTHOR'S NOTE

*"It takes nothing to join the crowd.
It takes everything to stand alone."*
~ *Hans F. Hansen*

When people ask me what I do and I tell them I speak with animals, one of two things will happen: they either make a beeline for "that thing they left in the car" or they will stick with me, intrigued to learn more.

Walking a road of difference and challenging the consensus is not always an easy one, but considering the global population of cats and dogs being kept as pets is well over 800 million, that is a lot of animals needing their voices heard.

Fifty and a bit years ago I was growing up in a small country town in Western Australia having enlightening conversations with dogs, sheep, birds, snakes and anyone else that had something to say. As it happens, when school begins and your intuitive brain shuts down, so did the window close on my chats with animals. Fast forward to the age of 40 and the animals had decided it was time for those windows to be lifted, so in the early hours of the morning, throngs of animals would push into my sleeping camera lens asking me to wake up. And while these daily visits did literally wake me up, their request was more along the lines of CPRing my overly hibernated intuitive communication abilities.

Their words were short and very clear. "Help us", they'd say. Two words that carried so much weight. It wasn't the words so much as the feeling of helplessness and despair that came with them and I knew I had to do something.

What I didn't know was this would be a turning point to one of the most meaningful periods of my life. After decades in the logistics and construction industries, talking to animals wasn't high on my list of things I might take up, but it seemed the animal collective had bigger plans than I did. Within a few short weeks the 2 a.m. "help us" wake up calls turned to the crystal-clear voices of animals in my ears as I'm going about my day.

"Hey lady, get out of the way," shrieks the parrot screaming an inch past my nose while running through the bush.

"Where's the privacy?" from the black French Bulldog as I watched him pooping out the front of his house.

"Can you throw me the ball?" asks the bored Border Collie as I walk by his gate.

"I love you, but you talk too much," complains my own cat trying to sleep while I'm chatting to him.

"The fish are oily from the boats and we're always feeling sick," says the Pelican eyeballing me on the Swan River.

"I'm a legend," responds the rather large dog being told by his struggling young walker that he's "a stupid dog".

I heard it all loud and clear and it was becoming more and more evident that animals have a LOT to say about everything and if you open your doors to hear them, these conversations are an invaluable source of information.

Rommie Buhler

It was one of those times when I just knew what had to be done, so without waiting a single second I enlisted an animal communication mentor and started a business connecting people with their animals.

"My pet has anxiety" is by far the most frequent enquiry I have, followed by the question, "Why is my horse misbehaving?" and an endless scroll of questions around strange behaviours, depression, anger, in-house fighting, illness, disease, nutrition, end of life decisions, missing animals. On and on I could go; the list is endless.

My intention in writing this book is to offer readers a perspective on our animals' health from the animals themselves. Humanity is the greatest influence on their lives and it comes with great responsibility. I encourage you to read this book with a curious and open mindset of learning how we can all do better for the welfare of all animals on this planet we share.

I have written this book as a series of short stories in a way that I hope can portray how animals feel from an emotional and physical perspective. Because if you can fully know how your anxious dog Rusty feels when his insides quiver, his belly feels sick and his brain is so full of mental tension trying to work out how to make this feeling go away, you would want to do something about that. And when you fully understand that your horse Sticks feels like he has a hot poker stabbing into his lower back when you're riding him and it hurts him to have you there, you would want to stop riding him and get help. When you fully feel and know when your cat Rastus has been in a traffic accident and is not wanting to be euthanized because there are options available to heal her, you would want to find the Chiropractor she's asked for.

The characters and events in these stories are a product of my imagination that have been inspired by the thousands of clients I have communicated with over the years as well as my own experiences with animals. Throughout the chapters you'll hear from a variety of different perspectives, including animals and their owners. My goal is that the different voices shared here will help you understand how the animal of that story feels physically and emotionally from their point of view as well as appreciating the struggle of their owners when they are unable to get to the bottom of a health or behavioural problem.

At this point I feel I should throw in a Disclaimer that this book is in no way a substitute for professional Veterinary care. My choice will most always be a Holistic Veterinarian; they are my first port of call when it comes to my own animals' health concerns.

I will be forever grateful to the animals for their teachings, wisdom and patience and for giving me the platform to be their voice. May this offering help build stronger and more connected relationships between people, animals and indeed all of nature. I invite you to sit back and read these stories and enjoy a small selection of what our animals have to say.

Rommie Buhler
Brisbane, Queensland

Where it all began in the Central Wheatbelt, Kondut, Western Australia.

INTRODUCTION

*"How it is that animals understand things I do not know,
but it is certain that they do understand.
Perhaps there is a language which is not made of words and
everything in the world understands it.
Perhaps there is a Soul hidden in everything and it can always
speak, without even making a sound, to another Soul."*
~ Frances Hodgson Burnett

I heard her coming before she came into view as the cat door thugged into violent swings behind her.

Purposeful, stompy cat steps followed by a rocketed pool of pink, sticky chuck lies swirling at my feet.

As a general rule, anything resembling an oozy mass of mucous sends me into a nauseating state of dry retching, but since I had asked all my hairy four leggeds to deliver news of any altered states in their health in a way that I could see it, I needed to "man up" and take a good look at this glop. Regurge with a dose of pink could well be blood—and blood outside the body isn't always a good thing.

It had been a while since my last tête-à-tête with Rizzy so I dialed in her telepathic number for her to show me that recent flooding had brought to the earth's surface toxic chemicals used to strip paint from a repurposed deck. Every day she would linger under this shady sanctuary, chase the odd bug and chew on the long grass growing underneath. What I didn't know was that eating this grass tainted with poison and grooming herself post lazing across this toxic dirt was making her very, very unwell.

A trip to the hardware store to wall off that kitty kat oasis and a series of (all clear) blood tests resulted in a rapid return to good health.

If I couldn't ask her the question and hear her answer, would I have known what to do with her? Considering her Vet report came back with a shiny gold star. That doesn't at all need answering, but since I asked the question, the answer is absolutely not. She was fatigued, vomiting pink (more than once), was eating little and she was clearly not on her game. I would have been panicking and paranoid and if she'd died on my watch; I may well have been writing this ridden with guilt.

If you read with enthusiasm beyond that piece about dialing the telepathic number, it's a good sign you're ready to at least consider the idea of *loving your pets well*.

We don't know what we don't know is a well-used expression and this very much applies to caring for an animal. Most of us learn from our parents (and how little they may know), the odd Vet visit for that one particular problem or a conversation with a friend that may have had an issue with their pet.

It is a huge responsibility to care for an animal and they need us to do our utmost to get it right.

They need us to stop guessing.

They need us to know the many solutions to the problems as they arise.

Rommie Buhler

And the humans need to stop feeling guilty when something goes awry— because it does and it will.

We are killing our animals with our lack of insight and education and it's time to change it up!

Yes, I said killing. Harsh word isn't it! I have done it myself so before you go and get all name-cally on me, do know that I am no Puritan when it comes to successful pet care. I am also writing this as a reminder to myself of the opportunity to help my own current and emerging pets to live long, healthy and happy lives (Did you know cats can live into their 30s?!).

Animals can hear you; they understand you and they are constantly communicating with you using this silent language of telepathy. It's the same language you use when you send over that unspoken request to your bestie to "bring the chocolate when you come over tonight" and, voila, in they rock with the block.

This is my 18th lifetime communicating with animals. That fat, pink, sloppy tongue that slobbered across my eyes when I was 2 years old was followed by a loud, two-year-old giggle and the question, "Cindy, why are you licking my eyes?" To which she came back with, "I'm cleaning you". Followed by more of my childish giggles.

From the snake slithering from the house to the shed telling me not to be scared he was just "going over there" and wasn't going to hurt me to the spokes-sheep asking me to "not let them be put on that truck" and many more stories of the same.

I am on a mission, my animal-loving friends, and quite simply that is to educate, inspire and motivate those of you that have animals in their life to uplevel your relationship with them, to know them on a deeper level, to be more present with them, to care for them with conscious attention, to communicate with them so you both understand each other and to love them into living a long, happy, engaged and meaningful life.

It is true that animals experience emotions and as such it is imperative that we look beyond the physical when seeking to understand how to help them live well. What I have discovered over the years is there are numerous simple, yet extremely effective solutions to many of these problems, many that cost you nothing and you can learn yourself. There are many aspects to an animal's life, their journey and healing so of course not all problems can or will be fixable, but you must at least know what is possible. Let knowledge be your superpower and fill your animal wellness toolbox with every piece of "how to, where to, what to" you can get your hands on.

There are a number of problems I see show up time and time again and I have selected some of these to share with you in story—from the perspective of the animal, the animal's guardian or that of the animal communicator. A book of fiction based on a blend of real-life clients including my own experiences with unconscious and uninformed animal parenting.

These stories are brought to you from my perspective as an Animal Communicator and are not intended to be shared from a science-based viewpoint.

Are you with me?

If it's a hands-down *awesome*, let's crack on...

...turn and learn readers!

In this first story I address a problem I see often—rescue animals with anxiety. Come and meet Norman, the repeatedly rehomed,

Rommie Buhler

highly anxious, rescue dog. As you follow his story you will understand how this traumatic start to life made Norman feel. And without giving too much away, you will also discover how Norman found his inner calm, peace and his forever home.

1
NORMAN HAS ANXIETY AND A NAME CHANGE

"With every animal, you have to build its confidence around people because people do some crazy and stupid things."
~ Ian Dunbar

And there I was, lost, scared out of my wits, walking aimlessly down a moonlit dirt road with nowhere to go.

Where was I? Nothing was familiar.

How did I find myself in this predicament, again! It's the third time in 12 months I've been kicked out of a Foster home. Only an hour ago I'd been helping Red with his new Lego build; the next minute, Mr. Jenson was yelling at me to get in the car. *NOW!* Red's sobbing—he doesn't want me to go—he'd finally found a friend. He was a shy boy and he didn't make friends easily. They'd moved more times than he cared to remember, but this was apparently going to be a long-term stay. His dad had promised and to prove he was serious, he contacted the local Foster Agency and brought me in.

I was pretty shy myself so we had something in common right off the bat. No-one seemed to like me much. I don't know why; I was a quiet-natured boy and kept to myself most of the time. Adults are confusing though, aren't they. They want you around and then they get mad and want you to "get out of my sight".

The last home I was in, Desiree—all the others called her Desiree so I did too—would chase us all around the house with a hair brush. *Oohhh* that hurt when she landed that across the back of your head. The kids would be crying all the time there. I'd had enough after a while so I took off.

Haaaaghhh, she was scary. I was happy to put her in my rear vision mirror!

The thing is, I genuinely thought she liked me; she was just in a spot of bother with her house payments and she'd just lost her job. She was nasty, but she was Desiree, the head of our unruly house. And so, after a few days I went back home. I forgave her, you see. It's easy for me to forgive because I'm always seeing the good in everyone. I know it doesn't make a lot of sense, but I think she needed me and I couldn't abandon her like that. And I was hungry, oh *man* was I hungry. All I'd eaten was half a burger I'd found in someone's bin up the street.

When I walked through the door, she was madder than I'd ever seen her; one look at her pinched, crimson face and I knew I was in for it. She was yelling at one of the kids when she spots me—and that was it. She went crazy, throwing anything she could lay her hands on. I ducked and ran, but not before being clipped on the chin by something hard—the pain was so hot I started seeing stars. My insides were shaking like a leaf.

Rommie Buhler

While I'm standing there trying to regain my balance, she walks over to open the door, looks me dead in the eye and says, "Get out of this house and don't you EVER step foot inside this door again."

I hesitated, thinking she was possibly overreacting.

"NOW", she booms.

I gave her my best big sad eyes, but she wasn't having it. She pushes me out the door with a "Get out!" and kick in the butt. And no food. Still no food. My stomach was going to start eating itself it was so hungry.

So there I was, walking the neighbourhood hoping she'd come find me when a car stops and a voice asks me if I'm lost.

That's a stupid question, I think. Of course I'm not lost, I'm waiting for Desiree to come to her senses and get me.

I'm a pretty smart guy—why does everyone think I'm lost! While I'm standing there wondering when they were going to leave, the man gets out and offers me a sandwich. *Oh, yes sir, please may I have that sandwich.* I was reminded of that hollowness in my belly.

He gives me the sandwich and tells me, "Get in, I'm taking you home". I clamber in the back seat, ready to go home, but we're heading in the wrong direction. This isn't the way home! I feel sick, this isn't right, where is he taking me?

As we pass street after street, I see an all too familiar sight. My stomach churns; I'm back here again. The joint they stick all the bad ones together. The reprobates no-one seems to want. This is the Foster joint—it's so busy and the constant comings and goings and incessant noise are unbearable. My nerves are a jangle; I can feel my innards tremble.

I let out a despondent sigh wondering what was to become of me. How long would it be "this time" before I get billeted out to my next home. I collapse exhausted on the bed and fall asleep with a heaviness in my chest that would sink a ship. It's the first time I've allowed that gnawing feeling I try so hard to push away and hope isn't really true, but in this moment, I know it is—no-one loves me!

Tap tap tap. Tap tap tap. There's a noise just outside my periphery beckoning me to wake up. I crack an eye to see a pencil-thin, pasty-skinned man tapping on the wall staring down at me. He smiles in what I guess is meant to be a friendly way, but I was miserable, not to mention uneasy and scared. And hey, it's not like he was going to want me; no-one else seemed to think I was good enough for them. So I sat there, motionless in the corner tracing his movements with my eyes.

Apparently, I was wrong! He shakes a handful of papers my way tells me to come along and off I go again on my way to my third home. I stared out the window in silence, wondering if this would be my final home. I breathe out wearily. The hope that someone would love me for who I was and let me stay was becoming a remote illusion of an idea.

He seemed nice enough. He talked all the way to his house. I didn't understand who or what he was talking about, but I'd learn soon enough.

As we pull into the driveway, I see a face peering out an upstairs window. A face full of sadness; he looked lonely, I thought.

The man opens the door and I can feel the change immediately—the weather's gone from warm with a light summer breeze to 50 below zero and frigid. I was instantly anxious, my stomach once again in knots.

"Boy", he yells, "get in here". The face in the window appears in front of me, his head hanging, staring at the floor.

"Look at me," he speaks frostily at "Boy". He lifts his eyes but doesn't move. I watch, realising I'm holding my breath waiting for what happens next.

"Norman, Red. Red, Norman."

"Give Norman some food, then go to your room until I say you can come out." He has a tone of icy hatred. I feel my innards trembling again. Something feels wrong here.

The man turns on his heel and stalks off to who knows where and it's just me and Boy. Or Red as we now know. It's awkward and clunky, but we manage to find some quiet ease between us.

Man spends his days drinking, yelling at us to stop doing whatever it is we're not doing and most days we get a good belting as he gets more and more drunk. We are each other's security blanket, spending our time fearful of what might happen next.

We're bound to Red's bedroom unless the Man needs us to buy him food or booze, then we're allowed out. It's a long walk to the shops and it feels good to stretch the legs.

We'd got ourselves into some sort of routine—if you could call it that—and then it happened.

We were quietly playing— we'd get beaten if we made noise because the Man hated sound of any kind—when I knocked over the bookshelf. It hit the ground with a crash. We transformed into instant statues praying the Man was too drunk to hear. Holding our collective breaths, we waited in hope. Our hearts sank as we heard his thundering footsteps boom up the stairs.

The door flies open, smashing into the wall and there he stands with fists clenched and eyes as wild as a bobcat. He glares at me bellowing that I get in the car.

"You", he pokes the air at Red…. "I will deal with you when I get home."

My heart is pounding a hole in my chest as the terror slices through my body. I find Red's eyes as I'm dragged out by the scruff of my neck to the car, neither of us knowing what each other's fate would be.

I'd lost track of time and I had no clue where I was. I'd slept on the streets many times in the past, so I should have been used to it, but I always felt jumpy and nervous. When you're on the streets, you're always sleeping with one eye open.

Click, click, click, click, click. The sound of footsteps on the sidewalk, every step closer to my secret spot. I'm hiding under a piece of cardboard and thought I'd done a good job of covering myself from sight, but those red glossy, high heeled shoes are stopped right in front of me. My heart's starting to race again and I feel panic rising.

"Be still, be still", I coach myself. "Don't move— she won't see you."

"Hi there, little man."

Too late. Damn it, she's seen me.

She leans down and removes my cardboard fortress.

So exposed, I think to myself.

She talks softly to me. Her voice sounds like a soft blanket. I catch myself starting to relax and then quickly tense back up preparing to do a bunk…. but this blanket voice… it's doing something weird to my brain. I can't think straight. My body softens and I think about coming closer.

Don't forget, she's one of those adults. I regather myself and remember where I am. I can't let that voice trick me. I reverse my butt back closer to the wall behind me, but there's nowhere to go— I'm cornered. My mind races; my eyes dart to escape points. I see the gap, commit and go for it, but she's quick— she's got me around the neck. I was ticked off and scared in the same breath and tried to bite the hand that was holding me tight.

She drags me kicking to her car and we're on the way. I don't know to where, but I'm starting to panic at what's coming. As my breath escalates and gets more and more haggard, she talks to me in blanket voice promising everything is going to be okay. *Yeah lady, I've heard that before. They all promise.* And a funny thing happens, I hear her breathing get really, really slow and metronomic and I feel mine doing the same. All the muscles in my body start to melt like warm honey and my eyes droop. My body's relaxing while my mind fights with what I know: that adults are mean and they can't be trusted. My mind is strong and I can feel my heart rate start to crank up again; my breathing becomes rapid and everything spins. I start to black out… the blanket's speaking.

"Come on little guy, we're home now, out you get," she says. "Let's go eat, you must be starving."

"Home". I was confused. *Home. What's home?* Didn't you need to fill out paperwork to go home? I didn't have a home. How was this home? So many questions.

The lady in the clicking shoes that speaks like a blanket walks me inside. The fire's on— it's the warmest I've felt since the Man dropped me on the side of the road. It's warm and homely and there were some seriously good smells coming from the kitchen. It reminded me how hungry I was. Meals were few and far between lately.

The warm blanket brought me the most delicious meal I'd ever eaten in my short life. I could feel myself let my guard down—just a little—but *no, NO you need to stay alert. Norman, you must stay vigilant.* I ran and backed myself into a corner. I couldn't trust her. I had to get to safety. Oh, how I hated feeling so sick in my stomach all the time.

She spoke softly to me and asked me what my name was.

"Norman," I said.

I don't think she heard me because she told me she was going to call me Stanley. I thought that was weird— I had a name and then she was giving me another one! Adults were not only mean; they were also strange.

But I liked her soft voice and I didn't mind Stanley either, so I decided that would be okay.

She called herself Mum so I called her Mum too. Made sense, if that was her name.

Nights turned into days, days into weeks, weeks into months and still I was here with Mum. Every day I waited to hear if I'd done something wrong, to be taken for a drive and dropped off to fend for myself again. But it didn't happen. She just loved me. The problem was I didn't know how to be loved, I didn't trust anyone—I kept waiting to be rejected and abandoned.

My heart so wanted to believe I was with Mum in this homely home forever, but every time she furrowed her brow or opened the door, I just knew I was a goner. I'd found a hideout spot for when she went out and I'd burrow myself in there to try to help me feel safe and stop shaking until she returned.

And then something happened. Mum brought this lady home with her one day and off we all went to the lounge room. Mum didn't have many friends over so this was a bit odd. She seemed nice enough and Mum liked her so I figured if she did then so would I.

She sat on the seat opposite me, but real close. She was way too into my space and I started to panic. I could see her hands coming to my face and I ducked for cover. The problem was she had one of those blanket voices like Mum and that made me feel calm and sort of okay like everything would be all right.

She told me she wanted to touch my face, but it wouldn't hurt—she was helping me to feel safer in my body and I could stop worrying in my guts. I just sort of went along with it. I'm pretty sure I was hypnotized as I couldn't seem to move.

One of her fingers is doing this tapping thing on my face and she starts saying these really weird things. "Even though I, Stanley, feel abandoned and rejected, I love and accept myself," she says.

What is this strangeness? I think.

Tap, tap, tap on all different spots on my body… it goes round and round and round. I start to feel relaxed. The permanent grip on my tummy is releasing for the first time since… well, since forever.

My eyes get heavy and I yawn. So relaxing. I groan in a satisfied sigh and fall deeper into a peace I've never known.

She's still tapping, but the words have changed. They don't really make sense, but I'm beyond caring about that now; I'm feeling more and more confident and comfortable.

".... I am confident, courageous and full of love. I am a great guy."
"I know I deserve love. I'm accepted and respected in my house."
"I am fearless, I am a good boy.".

Sighhhhhh. Deeper we go. Oh no, I can feel even my butt relax into a sigh of stenchy whiffs.

Sorry, lady. Can't help it, I think without trying to stop it.

I don't know what this tappy thing is, but I'm calmer and more relaxed than I have ever been. I don't feel the need to hide, my tummy's stopped its relentless, anxious quiver, my hips and hind soften and my tail comes out from between my legs and for once I feel like I belong somewhere. I am happy. I am happy for the first time ever. I look over at Mum and feel a desperate urge to thank her for loving and fixing me. I fly off my seat and launch myself at her, wrapping my strong Stanley Boy arms around her neck and cover her face with my biggest, sloppiest full of love licks a good dog could possibly give.

Her face is wet and I don't know if she meant her eyes to leak, but I can tell she's happy, too.

She puts her hands around my face and kisses me all over. She tells me I'm in my forever home and she loves me. No-one's ever told me they loved me before. I send her my biggest feeling of love I can do and curl up on her lap for the most full and restful sleeps I've had in my whole 12.2 months of being alive.

Anxiety is one of the top problems for my clients across practically all animals. If we talk about dogs for a minute, a study from the University of Helsinki in Finland[1] found that of 13,700 dogs studied, 72.5% of dogs expressed anxiety type behaviours. That is a huge number of dogs under stress.

Anxiety for an animal is a terrible feeling; it's like their insides are on a never-ending cycle of quiver and quake. There are many things you can do to help your animals with anxiety and it is worth investigating because I can tell you now, they do not want to feel like this at any time, let alone 24 hours a day, 7 days a week.

You will find a list of some of the more common tools and techniques I have recommended at the back of the book in the "33 Things Our Animals Need Us to Know" section. One thing I have noticed with people is they don't persevere with a treatment plan and jump from one thing to another if there are no results within a few days. Commit and be consistent. You may also find a combination of these protocols together will be more effective in healing your animals. For example, Emotional Freedom Technique combined with Tellington T. Touch and Flower Essences can bring about great results. Like people, animals can have many layers to peel back. It is not easy— the deeper the anxiety, the more difficult it will be to shift—but with kindness and patience you may just find a path to the other side.

---

[1] Milla Salonen, Sini Sulkama, Salla Mikkola, Jenni Puurunen, Emma Hakanen, Katriina Tiira, César Araujo & Hannes Lohi. Prevalence, comorbidity, and breed differences in canine anxiety in 13,700 Finnish pet dogs. Article Number 2962 (2020), 5 March 2020.

2
VELVET ROSE GOES ON A HUNGER STRIKE

"The only Bit a horse needs, is a Bit of understanding."
~ Carlos Tabernaberri

BOB OMAHA WILSON

If I was honest with myself, I was feeling disheartened and I couldn't put my finger on why. I'd been unsettled for six months and that part of me that knew things I wasn't ready to see yet was pestering me to look for something. The problem was, I didn't know what that something was. All I knew was horses were my life and at this juncture even that wasn't enough.

"You ready, Velvet Rose?" I asked aloud, sighing with a heaviness I couldn't shake.

It was a statement more than a question as she was tacked up and ready to get to work.

My first memory of sitting on a horse was well before I could even walk. I know that sounds early to remember something, considering that was 65 years ago, but for some reason I have an excellent memory of my childhood.

Ivan Omaha Wilson, my father, was a farrier and was determined I follow in his footsteps, so he had me around horses the minute I was born and home from hospital. I did follow his path for a while, but my interest was more in training horses than shoeing them, so I found myself a job as a farrier with a trainer. I became their head trainer early on and continued along until old Don passed away and then took over the business. That was 40 years ago and I've been doing it ever since.

I guess that's where I'm starting to come undone. Doing anything for 40 years is bound to lose its shine and it's a strange world this racing business. It's not all bad, but there are things I've seen that I can't unsee and there are things I know about I don't want to know about. It is a business after all and I'm near done with the business side of horses.

The dream of sitting on a fence rail with a cuppa watching retired racehorses with free rein to be horses tugged at the outskirts of my mind's desires. A vision that seemed to show itself often these days.

And then there's Velvet Rose. I have to tell you this horse has more potential than I've seen in all my years in the industry. She oozes quality and class and even if you didn't know what you were looking for, you would know she was something special.

She was sired by a track rockstar in his day, winning all but one of his 16 races and I should have been excited for what was to become of her; she was a powerful filly. Her training had been solid and she was muscular, sleek and calmer than a Zen monk—she was in unbelievable shape.

The truth is, I wasn't excited. I was... I was... I don't know what I was. Maybe I was sad for her; she was too young to start racing. I'd always felt that with starting them so early, but that's what you did so that's what you did until you no longer thought about it.

Rommie Buhler

Daniel had been working with her. He's one of the best in the business and she needed to get a good start. She'd been going well too and showing excellent promise until five weeks ago. Something's shifted and I don't know what.

While I might be known for my excellent memory, I have my quirks that most people find a bit mystifying. Like the acupuncturist I used the other day for Melisandé Rich who was struggling with colic and Nitro who was needing some pain relief. And the chiropractor and kinesiologist I brought in for Summer Cadence when she hurt herself getting out of the trailer last month. Oh, and this one, this is a beauty— I play them all music when they're agitated and hyped up; calms them right down.

So, when I say I don't want this broadcast to the racing world, I mean let's just keep it amongst ourselves. I've enlisted the help of Ben Hodge. He's a top young man, an exceptional equine mechanic and animal intuitive and he's heading this way to talk to Velvet Rose and work out how to help her.

And I reckon she's sad. Her eyes are flat, her head's low, she seems disconnected. When I watch her work, she's slow and unbalanced on her feet. The big thing I'm having trouble with is she's not interested in her feed box.

At the end of the day, all I am concerned about is young Velvet and it doesn't matter what people think, it's what's best for the horse.

Isn't that right, Ben! I call out as I spot him striding across the yard like he's meant to be somewhere.

"What's that, Bob?" Ben asks in his usual crisp, straightforward, no-nonsense style.

Out loud this time, I repeat, "Whatever the horse wants is what's best."

"Couldn't agree more," he says. He comes to an abrupt stop next to Bob, leaning, arms crossed on the fence.

"Who's our patient today?"

"Velvet Rose. Not on her game for some reason and I've got her down for her first race in Calgundah two weeks from now," I sigh heavily, feeling instantly pressured and exhausted.

"Right on." Ben shakes Bob's hand without wasting a second. "Let's go check her out and see if we can get some clues."

This is what I like about Ben. Less small talk and more business and I knew he was already connected in with Velvet Rose because he had that distant look about him that he gets when he's talking to animals.

We hadn't gone 10 paces when he stopped and started shaking himself off like a dog shaking off water. *All a bit strange, but I don't need to understand what this is all about, do I. If I didn't have an open mind, he wouldn't be here.*

"Bob, what blanket are you putting on this filly?" Ben asks.

My curiosity piqued, like something inside me knew what was coming next. I respond, "Using that new lightweight waterproof blanket. What're you thinking?"

That part where I get to feel what they feel isn't great for me, but I only get a mild version of what she'll be feeling. I feel electrical, like I'm being shocked. It's like I have fire starters going off in my brain and my entire body. It sure as hell doesn't feel good for her.

"I was just shaking it off, you might have wondered about that strange dance," Ben laughs at the thought of how he likely looked to an outsider.

"Is this synthetic, do you know?"

Scoffing at myself for being an easy sell for new trends, I inform Ben that it is the latest in synthetic blanket technology according to Ray at Equistore in Bundogan.

"Okay, that's gotta go right away. She's getting a blanket taser all day there and I can tell you it's draining her battery."

"Have you seen any fatigue lately, Bob?" Ben turned to look at me, already knowing what my answer would be.

I shake my head marvelling at how much this young fella knows without me having said a word. "I have, and that's another problem I wanted to talk to you about."

"Well, I'd say that's the blanket, but it's not the only thing. Give me a sec and let's see what else she's trying to tell me."

Ben closes his eyes in that way he does to communicate with Velvet Rose, feeling her power as he slowly smooths his hand down her neck. "She's impressive, all right," he says. "Who's she up against in Calgundah?"

"At this rate, it could be no one. We might scratch her yet. If she's up for it, she'll have a task with Tajan Redwing and Elwood Treadstone in the line-up. I'll call it at the end of the week. See what happens today." I feel a knot tighten in my stomach at the thought of Velvet Rose being pulled from her first race. In my 40 years I'd never had to do that and I feel like I'm failing her.

"Who's been training her?" Ben enquires, still with that glazed look.

"She's telling me the last few weeks she's being yelled at and it's a bit over the top. She feels like she's not good enough and she is also saying that she is letting you down. There's a strong connection between you and her and she's not living up to your expectations. Actually, I feel she's quite depressed. What have you noticed with her demeanour lately?"

A pause.

"Hang a minute, she's still talking," Ben puts his finger up to hold off Bob's response.

"Okay, something's changed here, she's saying. Everyone's acting angry and highly strung and there's no encouragement. This feels like it's affecting all the horses, not just Velvet Rose. There's a general sense of 'flatness' here with the people. And with that, I see she's not eating much or refusing her food. And that synthetic blanket is also contributing to her lack of appetite."

He pauses again for a moment.

"How does that fit with what you've noticed?"

Bob was momentarily lost for words. He hadn't seen Ben for almost a year and he'd forgotten how much he could garner from a conversation with his horses.

Eventually he managed to find his words and replied, "The blanket I never considered, but that timing works in with her change in mood and willingness to work. I've just taken the heavy one off which is a natural fibre so I'll put that back on. I've had her training with Daniel and he's a pretty calm young fella. I'll talk to him and see what he thinks of that."

He goes on.

"My expectations of her are extremely high. She's the horse I've been waiting for and she has huge potential. I have told her this every time I've been with her since she arrived."

Ben, drilling his eyes into Bob's to make certain he *hears* the importance of these next words, says, "She can '*feel*' that expectation from you and she's sensing enormous pressure to be better than she is currently capable of. She feels overextended."

Feeling mighty uncomfortable under Ben's stare, I shove my hands deeper into my pockets and look down at my boots, kicking holes in the dirt. I know where all this is coming from, but I'm not ready to face up to that thing I already know. So, with a shrug I tell him, "I'll have a think about that."

The problem is, everything goes a bit silent and I'm not good with complete quiet unless I'm on my own. I know he's waiting for a better answer than 'I'll have a think about it' and that quiet is starting to stretch into an uncomfortable silence. Before I know my mouth is moving, I hear myself admitting what I wasn't ready to admit.

"I suppose I've been pretty low myself and now that you mention it, I have noticed the crew here are much the same."

"She needs a lot more encouragement, Bob. And less bawling-out and demanding of her. Her energy is quite weak because she hasn't been eating. I know you have changed her food to see if that would help, but it's not the food that's the problem.

"Let me check in and see if there's anything else she needs from you," he says.

"Okay, right, she's also wanting her saddle checked. It feels loose and it's not sitting evenly which is placing pressure where it shouldn't and is causing pain.

"So, a few things to work with there, Bob." Ben lists off his fingers with each suggestion.

1. Change out that blanket.
2. Check with Daniel on how he's been training her; what's his energy like, what's his language like.
3. Encourage her more and let her know she's not letting you down, you're proud of her and want to work with her. Try and drop your expectations in your thoughts and actions, but also set this in your energy field if that makes sense.
4. And then keep an eye on that saddle. The food is fine. As she perks up, she'll start eating and she'll put weight back on and that saddle should fit again.
5. Any bodywork would be helpful and I think that needs to come from you. You need to reconnect with her again.
6. And Bob, if you're feeling flat and everyone else is the same, see what you can do to lift yourself and the others out of that.

"She's a beauty," he says. "Sort out these things and she'll be back and in form soon enough."

"Thanks Ben," Bob says, "Lots to think about there. I know you told me once before when there were problems with our animals to look at the people first. That had slipped my mind, but I think this is what you're saying today."

Bob gives Ben a pat on the shoulder. "Appreciate you coming out on short notice," he says. "You're a good lad."

Velvet Rose didn't go to Calgundah, but she sure did get to the next meet in Hydalborough. Came home 3rd in her first race by a hair's breadth.

Daniel did say he'd been getting more and more frustrated with her and thought he may have been yelling. Which in my mind means he was yelling—not too much 'may have' about that. We got the natural fibre blanket back out and although it's a bit heavy right now, it will work until I can get another lighter one. Now she's back eating, the saddle fits well and she is back to her old self.

I was a bit perplexed when Ben mentioned the crew were all flat, but when he left and I wandered around and thought about it, he was right. That came from me and that's not right for anyone. I made a big decision that day and for the first time in months I have a spring back in my step.

The business has been sold and in two months I will be moving and setting up a horse sanctuary in the Heldicon Valley. I will be taking in rescued and retired racehorses to rehabilitate and look after. I feel good about this decision and I know I will be seeing a lot of my horses again when they're ready.

Velvet Rose, you and I will meet again!

Have you ever been yelled at by someone— a teacher, parent, your boss? How did that make you feel? Animals can certainly test our patience, but every yell, name call and flash of anger directed towards them is one piercing stab in the heart after another and can result in depression, anxiety, wetting themselves, not eating, losing confidence or poor performance. I've seen it all and to feel that animal's emotions is gut-wrenching. If we look more deeply at what it is that's frustrating us, there will be a reason why they're doing whatever it is they're doing and it is imperative you understand where this behaviour is coming from and why. Only then can you know how to resolve this problem. The more you yell at your animals, the more they withdraw, the more frustrated you get, the more you yell, the poorer the behaviour and performance. It's a never-ending circle. An Animal Communicator can help you understand the "why" behind unusual and difficult behaviours. (For more information on how to work with me, see the section **Find Rommie Buhler Online** *at the back of this book).*

Static from synthetic horse blankets and synthetic bedding and clothing for our other animals is a very common problem that is terribly uncomfortable for them. The sensation of constant electric shocks running through their body and sparks inside their skull causes enormous stress and can affect behaviour, mood, energy, mental health, performance and overall health. A better option is to choose natural fibres for your animals.

3

SAM GETS A LESSON FROM HER BABY TIGERS

"Only if we understand, will we care.
Only if we care, will we help.
Only if we help shall all be saved."

~ Jane Goodall

Pipe down over there, you two. There are noises in this wall you might want to get yourself interested in knowing about.

And no, I do not want to get away from the wall and come over there for a pat. Do you not see my ears are otherwise engaged?

One minute they're calling me Little Tiger, the next they think I've got dementia because I'm focused on a wall that has creatures running around in it.

Humans! They're strange things, aren't they?

Now don't get me wrong, I love my people, and they'd know too because I've rubbed my spit on them enough times, but they're not a full bottle on looking after us cats. They've never had them before, you see, and they're making it up as they go along so I thought if I could explain a few things, they might be able to make a few changes in our home.

Before I get down and give you a lesson on what it takes to keep us cats happy, let me introduce myself.

I'll start with my name. It doesn't make much sense to me, but they liked it so it must be a good one. They called me Marbles because I looked like Dad's favourite doogs from when he was a kid. And it goes to show people are even more strange because they have names for things that don't even make sense, like doogs are marbles. Why can't marbles just be marbles.

I'm 4 years old and some would say mostly grumpy. What they don't know is, I'm not at all grumpy—that's just my look. Some might say I'm a finger overweight which I may just have to agree with because I've noticed when I jump down from my vantage points the cathunk noise is getting louder and heavier.

My Dad's name is Anthony; he seems to do painting things and collecting old chairs off the side of the road and hanging them on the wall in his office. I would say Mum is a cleaner at the Ritz Carlton as there is not a single thing out of place in this house—EVER! I hear people call her Sam so that would be her name.

To them my history is mostly unknown and to be honest for one second, if I may, what happened to me before today doesn't matter and it's also not so interesting, but I will tell you because people are curious and I want to get that out of the way before you ask.

Rommie Buhler

My cat Mum sort of belonged to Nigel the chicken farmer. I say sort of because she would spend most of her time outside, but on occasion and particularly when it was cold, she would be inside by the fire. She got into it with the neighbour's cat Smiggins and found herself pregnant with six small versions of herself. I had four sisters and one brother and we were born in a shed behind the chicken run.

Now, when Nigel found us, he wasn't too pleased and he collected us up without our mum and took us to a place where a lot of other cats lived. We barely had our eyes open so we mustn't have been more than a couple of weeks old which, if you know the order of things, that's about 10 weeks too early to be taken away from your mother's feeding pipes. That place was full of strange smells and a cacophony of noises which was very unnerving for us all so I don't remember that first stop too fondly.

A very nice lady by the name of Jan came and took me and two of my sisters home and fed us, but it seemed her seven other cats didn't want us around so we weren't there long. At this point my sisters Pins and Cecilia weren't feeling too good about this predicament so I took it upon myself to look after them and hoped that we would stay together.

Home three would see us with Michael the foster carer who seemed fairly decent. We were there for a short period before he remarkably had all three of us adopted into the same house.

And that brings us to now, living at the Ritz with Anthony and Sam, first time parents of their little tigers. By this time, we were 3 years old and hitting our prime and with their zero knowledge about how to manage baby tigers, they were in for a challenging start.

Anthony, who is mostly off in his own chair hanging world wasn't too phased with us and we all got along quite nicely. He'd leave the door open to his studio so we could amble in and out as we pleased, often spending hours on one of his classic chairs nailed up high on the back wall. Now this may have been one of his many unfinished artistic projects, but to us cats who like to be up high scoping from above that was a perfect spot to rest and observe the goings on.

A far contrast to Anthony, Sam who liked to make sure everything was under control and orderly had difficulty with the transition going from no animals to three cats seemingly overnight. I'd often hear Anthony say to her, "Let the cats be cats, Sam" when she'd complain about whatever the thing was that was causing her a sticking point.

She was the one that wanted us and our life lessons though so that's exactly what we were doing for her. Mum might call that punishment; we call it a gift and I'd like to dedicate the rest of this story to our Mum Sam to help her live in little tiger harmony.

MARBLES' LESSON FOR SAM: NUMBER 1

Lesson number one was to help her realise that cleaning the house within an inch of its life several times a day would result in three very stressed cats. Well, to be fair, Cecilia didn't seem to care so much, but that caused Pins and me great anxiety. All the walking around rubbing my glorious cat aromas on those surfaces made us feel comfortable and safe and she was quite unnecessarily taking them off. If she could feel that insecure quiver inside our body, she might understand the need to spray those scents back into our area.

MARBLES' LESSON FOR SAM: NUMBER 2

Not a lesson, but it sure would have helped Mum if she knew why she called us Little Tigers. Because the truth of the matter is we share nearly all our DNA with tigers and if she understood that better she wouldn't try and change the way we behave to suit her idea of what she wants from us. You might call it bad behaviour; we call it responding to our environment.

MARBLES' LESSON FOR SAM: NUMBER 3

Now this is something I would have thought Mum might have picked up on already since her hair is as immaculate as Switzerland. Dad, on the other hand, with his unkempt bird's nest may not have considered that having our hair out of place is literally quite irritating. So, if you pat us against our fur grain or you pat us one too many times and we bite you, that's just our loving way of saying, "Get your hands back in your pockets". On that note, Mum, you know how you want us to be huggy lap cats? Well, if you could wait for me to come to you instead of picking me up every time you walk past and patting me that would be cat-egorically good. No one ever really touched us when we were little so it's not so normal for us, you know. We are happy just being nearby if that would be okay.

MARBLES' LESSON FOR SAM: NUMBER 4

You might think we're here to taunt your cleaning mittens, Mum, but we're only suggesting that when you buy those plastic cutesy wootsy food bowls with high edges that our whiskers rubbing on the edges hurts and we need to throw our food on the floor. Don't think we don't hear your grumblings when this happens, but if you'd like us to scratch our claws on that shopping list blackboard you have in the kitchen so you know how that feels, leave a memo on the fridge. And one more thing… plastic has fumes that makes us sick and makes our food taste funny so if you can put our food on your Royal Doulton, that would be better.

OH, HERE'S A GOOD ONE MUM! LET'S CALLED IT MARBLES' LESSON FOR SAM: NUMBER 5

When we pee on the floor next to our litter tray, do know we're not trying to torment you. But gee willikers, that pellet business you put in there doesn't make our sensitive foot pads smile. And Mum— are you still there, Mum? Right, there's one more thing: one litter tray doesn't cut it for three of us. Can you try one for each of us plus a couple of extras. Why do we need extras? Well, you know we all like our own separate trays and then Pins needs one for pee and one for poop. And if it helps you understand, we like our trays much like your Ritz Carlton.

MARBLES' LESSON FOR SAM: NUMBER 6

You want your Little Tigers to live inside, Mum, and that's not really okay with us because we're built to hunt and chase and there's not much of that inside, but since we are here, we need to practice some of these things. You know that toy Dad made us last year? The one with the stick and the thing hanging off the end that ended up in the cupboard? Please get that out and play hunt the hanging bouncy thing with us. It's not that we're wired to tear around at 1 a.m. in the morning, but if there's energy to burn, we might get the zoomies. Go find that toy, Mum, and let's play chasey.

MARBLES' LESSON FOR SAM: NUMBER 7

Oh Mum, you know how you have a thing for cleaning? Well, I know that doesn't really include mopping up hoiked up fur balls so a good brush wouldn't go astray. It feels real good too, so go buy that brush that gets into the undercoat.

MARBLES' LESSON FOR SAM: NUMBER 8

Mum, this is a good one. I don't know if you moved that scratching post to the shed because it didn't fit with the interior design of the lounge room, but can you bring it back? That's where we get to keep our nails in good shape and have a good stretch. Maybe you could buy a few and put them where we all hang out—it might save the white leather lounge you don't seem to like us scratching.

MARBLES' LESSON FOR SAM: NUMBER 9

Listen up, Mum, I've got some good news. The house café is tops. Those little pieces of raw chicken wings are the best and that other stuff you give us, you know the one that is the same word for a spew—is it barf? That's real good, too; we like that. Makes us feel full and gives us lots of energy to play hunt.

MARBLES' BONUS LESSON FOR SAM

Mum, you're doing so well I thought I'd give you a bonus lesson. You know that window we look out of from that cupboard in the lounge room? Can you open that so we can get a niff of all those good smells and fresh air out there? And while you're at it, I was thinking if you're going to do that, you might as well hang a bird feeder in that big tree we can see from that window. That can be like our very own live television.

I know I'm asking a lot Mum, but all we really want for you is to know us better because then you won't get so frustrated with what we're not doing right.

Mum, are you still there?

Mum!

Don't cry, Mum, it's only because you don't know what we need, but now you've got Marble's Top 9 things, plus that extra bonus I gave you. You're a full cat bottle.

Don't feel guilty, Mum, it's okay. We're okay.

And Mum, one more thing. I was wondering if you might need some therapy on your cleaning obsession?

Where did you go, Mum? What are you doing in the bedroom? Oh, please don't cry Mum. Here, let me lie on your fragile heart and purr you some healing.

Mum—

Are you a cleaner at the Ritz Carlton?

> *In my opinion, cats are very misunderstood animals and I encourage all cat people reading this to learn more from the many cat behaviourists available globally. I've heard more than once, "Cats aren't dogs," and while that's an absurd comparison, some people want from their cat what a dog gives to their people. The biggest complaints I hear about cats is they're not affectionate and they bite or scratch when they're patted.*
>
> *Cats are hypersensitive; they can't handle being patted repetitively. This may result in biting or scratching, but it is not because they're aggressive, that's their language for "enough now". Of course, all cats have different levels of tolerance, so one you might pat until you've had enough, while the other you may get three strokes in and be rewarded with their fangs in*

your arm. Learn to understand your cat's sensitivity and their manhandling threshold.

Cats can also love you from "just over there", so if you want them to be lap cats and they're not, you must be okay with that. I have noticed the less they have been handled as kittens, the more independent and less wanting to be touched they are. And in case you're not aware, cats share over 95% of their DNA with tigers so they are literally little tigers! If their personality doesn't allow you to pick them up and stick them in your face, don't do that. They will come to you if and when *they* come to *you*.

One of the greatest problems from a cat's point of view is they are so incredibly BORED! If they are outdoors, they can be more easily stimulated with sights, smells and creatures scuttling in the garden. Indoor cats have very little stimulation and they are desperate for it. It doesn't take much to play with them. Let them practice their hunting and chasing skills with that mouse or bird thing on the end of that stick you've shoved to the back of the cupboard. They need to be mentally nourished (and they need to move).

Learn to understand your cats, feed them a species-specific diet, play with them and, most importantly...

LET CATS BE CATS.

4
MR. BANKS DETECTS A PROBLEM

"Many dogs grow up without rules or boundaries. They need exercise, discipline and affection in that order."

~ Cesar Millan

STARKY

I step into the shed for the third time today and for the third time I don't remember what I am doing there.

Come on Starky, you've got this, I coached myself. *You came in here for…*

I wait expectantly, anticipating the blank to be easily filled with that elusive answer, but I just can't seem to pull it in. I sigh heavily and rub my aching neck ignoring the dull and distant headache that seems to be a constant these days.

At least I remembered it was my third attempt, I laugh nervously to myself.

You might wonder why I'm feeling anxious. I'm not the only one that forgets what they're doing, am I. I mean, my sister Sarah would forget her own name if she wasn't careful. I reckon it sounds like a family problem. Well, at least that's what I'm telling myself.

"Starky! Give us a hand, would you mate."

Ahh, a distraction from my thoughts. Perfect timing.

"Be right there, Rich," I yell out as I lock the shed and head next door to friends and neighbors' Rich and Serena Sewell. A quick "give us a hand" always ends up with a beer and BBQ and that's about what I needed today.

I hear Banks inside crying and scratching at the door trying to come in. I pause, wondering if I should take him with me.

Not today, I think. He's been damn hard work these last few weeks whining and pacing and carrying on; I needed a breather from this erratic behaviour.

I fed Banks, grabbed a beer and swung up the multipurpose gate we'd built between our houses— a fencing masterpiece Rich and I came up with 10 years ago. This creative genius opens as a shortcut entrance or folds down into a four-seat table. Makes the social functions a whole lot lighter to carry!

I smile to myself as I think back to happier times.

BANKS

My full name is Mr. Edward Cunningham Banks, but you can call me Banks. You can also call me, "You're A Good Boy", which Dad calls me on a regular basis. It's not that I think he's forgotten my real name, I just think it must be easier to remember or something.

Rommie Buhler

I'm 7.2 years old, a Boxer X Street Dog and if you don't mind me saying so, I am handsome. Another very important factor is that I'm as funny as hell. It's my number one job, you see. I need to help my Dad when he slides into those dark places he gets himself into.

Dads and their dogs! What can I say—they are like two links in a chain.

I picked him out when I was 6.3 weeks. You see, he literally tripped over the fence and landed face first into a puddle of mud and it was me that saved him. Yes sir, I did. I squirreled through my five brothers and one sister and pulled on his shirt until he was able to stand up—but not before catching my full and very serious attention. I mean, he was going to be my dad and it was crucial he remembered me for my pick up date in 5.7 weeks' time.

Now what you have to understand about us dogs is we know more about you than you give us credit for. We know when you're happy, we know when you're sad, we know when you need to stop and relax, we know when you shouldn't be doing that thing you're about to do that can hurt you, and we know when you're sick.

The problem is when we're trying to tell you that thing we know that you don't know yet, you don't hear us. Can you imagine talking to someone all day long and they never hear you? It's a very frustrating thing, that is.

In fairness to Dad, he always picks up when I'm hungry. One sharp bark and dropping my food bowl as loud as possible always sparks results. Usually preceded by a: "BANKS, Put. That. Bowl. Down. NOW". It works though and you gotta do what works, don't you.

Coming back to Dad and noise. Well, we weren't so much talking about noise, but I can tell you this, it can make him real cranky. And lately I have been making him a lot ... shall we say, peppery.

It's important, you see, because I see what he can't and it's BIG. He needs to hear what I've got to say because this thing he's blind to will affect the rest of his life. So, I take it upon myself to go all out to get his attention. Normally I'm a chilled Banks that loves nothing better than to spread eagle on the lounge, but right now I've got work to do. I sit on top of him like I never normally do when he's on the lounge. I howl, stare him out and bark constantly.

Nothing. All he's hearing are dead ends!

So, I upped the ante and stopped eating. For someone that hoovers their entire dinner before the bowl's even hit the tarmac, I was certain that would get his attention.

Silence!

I whine. I pace. I bark. I bark. I pace. I whine.

I hear him telling Rich next door that I have anxiety.

Let me be clear with you. Mr. Banks does not have anxiety.

The only anxiety I have is Dad not hearing me and me running out of ideas on how to get this pivotal news across.

STARKY

"Rich, mate, what's happening over here? What's on the fix for today?"

"Ah, good, Starky you're here," the neighbour replies. "No fixing today, buddy. There's someone I want you to meet. I hate to be an arse, but Banks and his howling and barking is driving the neighbourhood crazy. Serena met this lady at some event yesterday and apparently, she can talk to animals. We thought she might be able to get to the bottom of this twist in Banks' behaviour so I invited her over."

"Haha, you're having me on aren't ya, Rich," I laugh. "People can't talk to animals, that's ridiculous. She's not some whacko, is she?"

"Could well be, mate," he says, "But I'm paying for it and if it can stop this racket I reckon it's worth a try. What do you say, can I bring her out?"

"Yeah, why not!" Starky snorts with laughter. "I need some entertainment and this is the funniest thing I've heard in a long time."

"Serena!" yells Rich, "Starky's here to see Emily. Can you bring her out?"

"Give her a chance, mate," he says. "You never know—it might help."

She walks out.

"Emily, good of you to come out," Rich says. "This is Starky, Banks' Dad. Starky, Emily."

"Hi Starky, nice to meet you," says Emily.

Starky, now curious, exclaims to Emily that she looks normal.

"What did you expect me to look like?" she asks.

"I don't know," he says, "But not like a regular person in the street."

Emily laughs. "Yep," she says, "I could be your neighbour and you'd think nothing of it. I run, sing in an 80s cover band and love a good coffee. Pretty normal, I'd say."

She smiles. "Now, you have a dog who you think has anxiety," Emily says. "Serena has explained he's been whining and barking more than normal, so let's see what he has to say about that. Do you have a photo of Banks?"

"I'm sure I have a photo on my phone," Rich replies. "But we're right through the fence—shall I bring him over?"

"No, that's fine," Emily replies. "A pic is enough."

Emily takes Starky's phone and stares intently at Banks on the screen.

Skeptical Starky raises his eyebrows and smirks at Rich, waiting for the show to start. He'd always thought Rich was a bit out there, but this was taking it to a whole new level.

Her question snaps him immediately out of his reverie.

"What's going on with you, Starky?" Emily asks. "I am getting shown your brain by Banks. Do you have headaches at the moment?"

Clearly shaken, but not wanting to let on, Starky dismisses this question and with a laugh says, "The odd headache, no more than usual. I thought you were here to figure out what's going on with Banks."

There is a hushed pause.

"Hmmmm," Emily says. "Banks is telling me he's trying to get a message to you. And I hear this has been for at least the last three, if not four weeks, would that be correct? Did his anxious behaviour start three to four weeks ago?"

"Ah, well, yes," Starky says. "That would be about right." He mumbles to himself. "It was before I came out of contract with the Renegades and started negotiations with the Sentinels… and that was four weeks ago. Now that you mention it, this was when the discussions with the Sentinels started." His voice trails off.

"That's interesting, Emily," Starky says, "You have my attention. What's wrong with him?"

"Just to explain, Starky, it's a bit like putting the puzzle pieces together," Emily says. "Sometimes it's very clear and simple and other times it's more cryptic. Banks will send me snippets of information through images, words or feelings and then with your help we can work on interpreting it together.

"What he's showing me here is him pacing furiously and whining and in my stomach, I feel sick and quivery like I have anxiety. This is not mine. It is his way of showing me how he feels by placing it in my body. I can understand why you think he's anxious. He is, but it's only because you're not hearing what he has to tell you and it's important to him."

Emily pauses for a moment.

"Let me ask Banks why he's showing me your head and headaches," she says. "Give me a sec."

Emily stares down to the left, her spot for talking to the animals and looks at Starky with a mixture of concern and kindness. She pauses, formulating the right words before she speaks.

Animals Speak

"Starky," Emily says, "I'm seeing Banks sniffing at your energy field. He's smelling a health concern that he is indicating is serious enough that he needed to 'act out' to get you to address this situation, before...before you make any rash decisions or it's too late to fix whatever is going on.

"Can I ask you, those headaches you have on the odd occasion—where do you think they've come from and have you seen anyone for them yet? He is showing me a dark shadow in the area of your brain. Does this mean anything to you?"

"Mate," Rich cuts in. "You hadn't mentioned these headaches have started again. What's going on with you?" asks Rich.

All eyes were now on Starky and the conversation was fully focused on this concern for his aching head. He was like a deer in the headlights. He was tired, scared and resistant to impart any further information.

There is power in silence. After a few minutes, holding his head in his hands, Starky says, "The headaches are hell, but it's not just that. I'm getting forgetful, my eyes are blurry and I'm always tired."

Deciding whether to continue, he whispers, "I missed the last two scans."

"Maaaatte," Rich says, "You've had *seven* concussions this season alone. You know what they said after that last knock! It's a risk to continue playing footy and you need a brain scan every six months."

Rich looked at his friend with concern.

"I know, I know," Starky says. "I missed the first one and felt okay. And the contract being drawn up with the Sentinels is all but signed off. I can't miss another season. It has always been my dream to play with my home club. I have to sign. I'm getting too old—no one else will pick me up."

Silence fell over the group, each lost in their thoughts.

"Would you like me to have a look at the possible outcome for you, Starky?" Emily asked. "Or at least check with Banks on what he thinks is the first thing you should do?"

She looked at him. "If this is potentially going to change the course of your life," Emily went on, "would you want to know what may happen if you continue being knocked out in your games?"

The questions hung in the air for what felt like an hour as Starky struggled with his internal argument. *Ignorance is bliss*, he thought. But, at the same time, *I need to know the effect this is going to have on my health and my lifestyle if I continue on.*

"Okay," he said, turning to Emily. "Yes. Let's hear what you've got to say."

Emily closed her eyes and became very still.

"Starky," she said, "You really do need to have that scan you've been putting off. This is what Banks has been trying to tell you. He will settle down once you have done that. You need to speak with your doctors about the consequences of continuing playing. The multiple concussions you have been subjected to over the years has the possibility of serious long-term effects on your health.

"There are difficult conversations and big decisions to make and only you can make those, but some decisions you can't make without first gathering all the information. Learn more about your situation, speak with your specialists and then project into your future health state and decide whether that is how you want to live your life in retirement. I see the memory loss, dizziness, headaches and frustration may get worse."

Starky sat in a state of shock. *This is not the afternoon beer and BBQ I thought I was coming to*, he thought.

BANKS

With a satisfied sigh, Banks settled down and slept for the first time in four weeks. His job was done!

> *I have had numerous experiences with (animal) clients smelling deficiencies (or excesses) in the body of such things as Vitamin B12, magnesium, salt, potassium, lead, mercury, Vitamin K, Vitamin C, etc. Illness and disease, including brain injuries, poor liver function, digestive disorders, eyesight and hearing concerns, blood disorders, etc have also shown up a number of times with both dogs and cats I have spoken to. Animals are trying to communicate with us all the time. If their behaviour seems irregular and there is no reason or cause that you can understand, pay attention to what is going on with you. Dogs are particularly good at detecting abnormalities in our energy field. The energy field is an extension of our body and illness, health imbalance, disease and emotional issues can show up here well before it manifests in your physical body. You may have heard of service dogs working with diabetics that detect chemical changes in the body. Dogs sense much more than we can possibly imagine so pay attention to them.*
>
> *In this story, Banks was trying to show Dad he had a problem that needed to be addressed. I have seen this often and the animal will usually exhibit a heightened state of anxiety when*

you are with them. If they are already anxious, this is not always easy to see, but if your animal doesn't suffer with anxiety and there is no valid reason you can see for this behaviour, it may be a message for yourself to follow up on.

You may have heard the expression anxious dog, anxious owner—animals often show us the things that need to be addressed by mirroring back to us an illness, injury, energy, personality or behaviour, etc. I've seen cats that overeat to highlight to their person they're eating too much; I've had dogs with spinal issues showing their person it's time to heal the emotions around a spinal injury accident. I've had animals with cancers that their person has, Dad with the limp in the left leg that was a tumour in the hip and dog with a limp in the left leg (not a tumour, but this limp was highly exaggerated until Dad discovered his tumour and his dog miraculously lost his limp). I've seen a grumpy horse, grumpy rider; cat with a broken right wrist, Mum with a broken right wrist and so on. It is not always the case that your animal is mirroring something to you—animals do have their own problems, but it is worth throwing the spotlight on what's going on with you.

Animals are like our very own life coaches; they show us how we're showing up to others. They're our greatest teachers and they're free—what more could you want! All you need to do is open your mind and heart to their wisdom.

5

CALENDULA SOLVES THE MYSTERY OF KALEENA GALE'S ODD BEHAVIOUR

"Horses have taught me a kind of meditation that's possible as you are acting as one and communicating instinctively without words."
~ Robert Redford

I think I'd almost hypnotised myself mucking out the stalls that morning—I'd lost all track of time. You know how you do that when you're doing something so often you stop having to think? I mean, raking out horse poop wasn't everyone's cup of tea, but I liked that time—I was by myself with the horses, it was quiet and I got a chance to take them through all my troubles. Because, as you might know, when you're a 13-year-old girl who's a bit of a tomboy, things can get tricky.

There's nothing wrong with being a tomboy, I don't think, but my mum tells me I should be like my friend Holly and act more like a girl. I don't know what that means when Holly rides horses like me and she doesn't mind being dirty. I suppose she does act a bit different, though. Holly has the mane of a black stallion and violet eyes like the night sky—she's pretty and everyone at school likes her. They swarm around her like she's some kind of god.

She has this way of walking—she glides across a room like she's hardly moving, yet there she is suddenly on the other side of the room. Me? You can hear me coming a mile off. Dad tells me I walk like an elephant. He's probably right. I am pretty loud. And I'm always late, so I'm mostly running everywhere I go.

I've got my own white-blonde mop, almost down to my waist, but it's not like Holly's who's silk black and always in perfect alignment. Mine's wild and never seems to sit in any place, let alone the perfect place.

Coming back to things being tricky for a long time—well, the problem is my name. You see, Mum helps people get healthy. She's sort of like a naturopath but she works with herbs. Thirteen years ago she'd had a miracle healing with this lady with the calendula flower. And since I was apparently a sort of miracle—I don't know why, but that's what they tell me. "Calendula," Mum says, "You were our miracle child." So, after that, she decided to call me Calendula. I mean, who does that? Call your kid the name of your miracle flower. Right from when I started pre-school, I was getting a hard time. They all called me the Flower Girl. Let me set you straight about one thing, when you're happy being a tomboy, you don't want to be referred to as the Flower Girl.

So, I say, "Please call me Cally—that's my name."

My dad's a farrier and puts shoes on horses and when he says it's okay, I go with him to his jobs. You know when you love something so bad you just want to be near it? That's how I feel about horses and when I'm with Dad, I'm also with horses.

I suppose that's what made me stick to animals for my main friends. They were much easier and didn't make fun of me.

We have horses—I already mentioned that when I was telling you about mucking out the stalls. We have two dogs, Rosie and Jerry, and we have three cats, Ginger, Nutmeg and Spice and we also have Magenta, our pig. When I'm not at school or doing homework, I'll be feeding, brushing, cleaning or playing with my animal friends. We spend a lot of time together. And you know, I always seem to figure out what's wrong with them. They sort of speak to me in a way. They do it to you too, right? Well maybe you don't hear them like I do, but they'll be talking to you all right.

Sometimes they show me pictures in my head when they want something. Other times I might just know something's not right. Like the other day when I was brushing Rosie, our Red Cloud, and I tied her to the post funny and it was hurting her neck. I was getting into the matted bits around her tail when all of a sudden, I had this urge to check her tie and I noticed it had twisted her neck on a freaky angle. She was breathing a bit strange and I knew it didn't feel good.

I feel things, too. Especially when they're not feeling right. And that's what happened that day when I was mucking out.

I was in a bit of a daydream and I heard the rumbling noise in the distance. My head shot up like a torpedo.

The Bus!

I was late. I was always late. I didn't mind too much, but it would be easier if I wasn't.

I dropped the rake and flew out of that barn like I had a rattlesnake in my pants. The bus was almost at my driveway and I couldn't seem to run any faster. Mr. Vernon was nice though and he always seemed to wait for me —even today when he got there before me.

He sighed and shook his head as he always did and tatted, "Cally, Cally, Cally, always late". I flew onto the bus, breathlessly wheezing, "Sorry, Mr. Vernon", as I always did and collapsed into my seat nearly sick trying to catch my breath.

I liked the bus trip to school. It was a full hour of being occupied with what was going on outside on the farms we passed. We were coming up to my friend Holly's place and I could see her out there jumping her favourite horse, Gee. Gee's not her real name; it's Kaleena Gale, but we just call her Gee.

It's a steep hill getting up to Holly's and the bus always bucked and banged trying to get to her stop. Which was good today because I knew something was off and I needed time to figure it out.

Like I said before, I don't know why, but I can sort of hear the animals talk to me. And I feel it too when they're in pain. I can't explain it, but I just seem to feel it in my own body where they're hurting in theirs.

I'm not full of myself or anything, but I must be alright at it because people seem to ask my dad if I can help them when their animals are sick or playing up.

I haven't seen Holly lately, but her mum told my mum she wasn't placing well at her events and Gee was acting up. He'd even started kicking out and had thrown her off a couple of times. They'd had the vet out three times and there was nothing wrong they could see. Mum said they would probably have to sell her. If I know

Holly, I know she would just die if that happened— she loves her horses more than anything else.

The bus chugged its way up Mount Binten and while I was watching Gee balking at jumps and throwing her head around in a fluster, I felt this stabbing pain down the bottom of my back. You know that flat part under your ribs, about where the top of your jeans sit? It hurt so bad I flinched and yelled out a bit. It's sort of a strange thing though because I don't really feel it like it's my own pain, but it still makes me wince. As soon as I've felt it, it fades right away so I don't mind too much. It's like I need to know where and what it feels like and once I do, I don't need to know any more. When I yelled out, I felt like my legs wanted to buckle under me, like I couldn't hold myself up and I was a bit uncoordinated.

I think she needs a Chiropractor, I thought. Well, they weren't really my thoughts; they were directions that I heard in my head for Gee.

There was a horse chiropractor in the next town— his name was Dr. John something-or-other. His surname was long and it never stuck so I just knew him as Doc John. I'd met him a few times with Dad when they were working on horses together. I didn't much like how he pinched my nose whenever I saw him, but he was really good at fixing horses. We'd had him out once when Magenta slipped and dislocated one of her knees. She was brand new again real quick after Doc John visited.

I could see Holly's shocked face as she heard the bus. She was like me—always late. I hoped she was going to make it; I wanted to tell her what I felt about Gee. We were getting closer to her stop and she wasn't there yet. I could feel my left foot start doing its tapping thing. It always did that when I was nervous about something.

I stretched my neck trying to see if Holly was coming back outside. *She's not going to make it*, I thought, *we're nearly there.*

Finally, I see Mrs. O'Dette and Holly run outside and get in their old beat-up blue VW Beetle. Gee and their old pony Rusket were left in a trail of dust as Mrs. O'Dette raced to the end of their pretty long driveway. I look at Mr. Vernon to make sure he's seen them. He was watching. *Good, he'll wait,* I thought. I let out a long breath, not realizing I'd been holding it. I needed to help her save Gee, so I had to tell her my thoughts.

Mrs. O slid to a stop and Holly opened the door and clambered out of the car all smiles and grace like she'd been waiting for the bus and not the other way around.

She threw her bag on and slid into the seat next to me with a mouth full of words that never seemed to have full stops or commas.

"Hi Cal, can't believe I nearly missed the bus again," she said. "Did you see Gee? She's really obnoxious at the moment. Mum and Dad don't know what to do. We've had the vet out three times and she's still not jumping properly. Do you think you could have a look at her?"

I can't write it the way she said it, but all of that came out in one breathless sentence.

"Hol," I said, "I think you need to get Doc John out. I feel sharp pain in Gee's lower back and it's like her legs and tail aren't plugged into her body. She feels real wonky and unsure of her movements. And she tells me she's a bit scared too. See if he can have a look and get her straightened out. She doesn't want you on her, Hol, it's hurting her a lot."

We sat silently for the rest of the trip. Holly was chewing her bottom lip, which she always did when she was stewing on something.

Rommie Buhler

I knew Holly pretty well; we'd grown up together right from when we were zero. We were born just one day apart and every year we shared a birthday together. And Dad worked on her horses so if we weren't at school together, I was at her house.

We were like yin and yang, me with my long white-blond shag pile, turned up nose and blue eyes—and her with her black hair, violet eyes and long, skinny nose. We were best friends and helped each other with everything.

She said she'd talk to her mum after school and see if they could get Dr. John over. She didn't want to wait another minute and none of them wanted to sell Gee. No one wanted to think about the consequences of that. Sending your horse away to another person just about makes me want to be sick.

Late Sunday afternoon, the phone rang out in the barn. I didn't pay much attention to it since no-one ever rang for me and the barn phone was Dad's work number. I could hear him mumbling to someone and then the next minute he's hung up and off grabbing his coat.

"Cally, get your shoes on, we're going for a drive," Dad says. "And grab a jacket, it's cold out."

I liked the sound of getting out. It had been raining and we'd all been cooped up inside since Friday.

"Where are we going?" I yell at him as I run around searching for my missing shoe.

"You'll see," he says. "Just grab a jacket and hurry up."

He's waiting for me out the front as I awkwardly try to run, put my shoes on and tie laces at the same time. *Next time I'll put both of my shoes together,* I grumble to myself as I jump in the truck.

It was still drizzling out and I'm watching the drops hit the side of my window when I see we're turning into the O'Dettes' driveway. I guessed Dad was coming to do some work. I hadn't noticed he didn't have any of his tools with him; I was just glad to be out of the house and doing something. And even better that I was going to see Holly.

"Cal," Dad says, "Look." He was pointing off to the left.

What I saw…

I was so excited and emotional at the same time. I mean, I wasn't sad, but tears were creeping awkwardly out of my eyes.

There was Gee floating around the arena like a silk ribbon. Holly was smiling so hard as we pulled up, I worried she might crack her cheek bones.

But I could feel it. Yes, I could feel it. The pain was gone! Gee's balance was back and her tail was up. She was going to be okay.

I flew out of the truck as Holly came sprinting over to give me the biggest hug. She was crying, I was crying— even Mrs O'Dette was crying and she never cries.

Dr. John had found the problem and fixed her right up. She wasn't going to be sold, but the most brilliant part was that Gee felt free again and she could get back to doing what she loves, competing with Holly.

In all the years I have been communicating with horses, I can say I have not seen a horse misbehaving for the sake of being disobedient. Behavioural issues for all animals can often stem from fear; the language we use can be confusing to them and create misunderstanding and then there's the physical illness, injuries and pain.

As I attract clients with anxiety, I also seem to draw in horses with lower lumbar, hips, withers and shoulder pain. While this is not always the problem, the majority of horses I see throwing riders, balking at jumps and generally being difficult to handle, are reacting to pain and fear of the physical weakness. As a medical intuitive I can feel what an animal feels in their body and lower lumbar pain ranges anywhere from very uncomfortable to excruciating.

All situations are unique, and as I mentioned there are many different reasons for behavioural changes in horses (and all animals), but there are many modalities of healing available to try before considering surgery (which is a last resort, in my opinion). I have found skilled Equine Vets, Chiropractors, Osteopaths, Mechanics, Bowen Therapists, Acupuncturists and various other bodywork techniques to be effective in treating musculoskeletal and neurological problems. I can also tell you that these horses do not want to be ridden under these circumstances. If you are competing your horse, it is important to step aside from your human wants and desires when your animal is in pain.

The majority of my horse clients are performance horses and have often had many homes. It is common to see problems with rejection and abandonment in these horses (and all animals being rescued or rehomed) which can show up as anything from fear and anxiety to depression. There are many things you can do for emotional problems in our animals, but one that I have found to be consistently effective is Emotional Freedom Technique (EFT). For more information about EFT, see the Resources section at the back of this book.

Other behavioural issues I see often come from saddles not fitting correctly (due to weight loss, using another horse's saddle or poor customising) or Bits being used (I haven't found a horse yet that likes a Bit no matter how many different versions you try). There are also issues with shoes, teeth, ulcers, loneliness, trust, poor handling, not wanting to compete in the discipline they are being trained for, or being stressed when they are rehomed when they are happy or losing friends that have been moved or rehomed.

Healing an animal of any emotional or physical concern can take time, effort, consistency, persistence, patience, respect and a whole lot of love. Provide them this and you will be rewarded with a healthier, calmer, happier and more connected animal.

6

WINNIE'S TICKET TO FREEDOM COMES UNDONE

"Way down deep, we're all motivated by the same urges. Cats have the courage to live by them."

~ Jim Davis

MAGGIE

It's 1:30 a.m. and I'm lying staring at the ceiling—again! The luxury of even one uninterrupted sleep was as slippery as an eel when my inbox was full with missing animals. If only my spirit FBI team wouldn't have this burning urge to converse at such uncivilized hours of the night. I watch the clock tick over to 3 then 4 then 5 a.m.

"Get up", my morning voice rasps to myself, "There's work to do."

"Five more minutes", I announce to no one in particular as I roll back and re-assume the sleeping position.

So comfortable, so tired and yet so awake. With considerable effort I groan myself into a sitting position and let my mind wander to today's client. Winnie had been missing for 17 days and I could feel her energy slipping. Wherever she was, Winnie's mum Janice needed to locate her before it was too late.

It was time to channel my inner sleuthhound and see what clues I could draw down. My night-time FBI session had shown me some very interesting leads to follow up on and time was of the essence with this furry client.

WINNIE

The window was half open. I knew that crack was my free pass to the world of exhilarating smells and chases.

You know when you're cooped up inside for days on end, eventually your body needs to get itself outside? Well, that's how I feel every day. See, the difference between you and me is you get to go outside… me? I've never been outside.

I have this spot on top of the lounge where I can see out the window. It's like joy and torture all at the same time. I see all the things I could be doing out there, but Mum says I might run off and get into trouble with traffic so I'm forbidden to go to that place my feline like body aches to be.

And if you were a cat, you'd know we need to chase things. Don't get me wrong, I love a lazy stretch out in Mum's sleeping quarters, but there are times I burn to get outside to climb trees and chase things that scuttle. I know you all hate me for that part, but you can't blame me, it's my wiring. I mean, when you look at it, it's the same as your instinct to eat— you can't control it, it just is.

Rommie Buhler

Now, back to my story of the open window. Every day of my three cat years I have fantasized about getting my toe beans on that garden patch I see from my lounge tower. The idea of it makes my body tremble with hope. Little did I know that today was going to be my day!

I float up like a cat ninja and get ready to settle into position for the day —two circles to the left, two and a half circles to the right and… wait, was that a breeze fluttering across my whiskers? I stop mid circle and become statue Winnie, curious and excited at the same time as I realise there is a window crack ready for Miss Houdini herself to launch through.

I erase all memories of Mum, with her stern voice telling me to "stay inside!" and I slip onto the windowsill to survey the scene for landing platforms.

My body shudders in anticipation as I line up the garden table perfectly positioned under my escape hatch. I land with the lightness a Navy Seal would be proud of. I've barely settled when I spot something scooting around the flower bed to my left. Every one of my silent chasing senses is pinging and I'm off like a shot.

Back, forth, up the tree, down the tree, across the sand patch, over the fence, run chase run.

I am so caught up in my chase I fail to notice Bandit, that ferocious dog from next door is outside.

He's coming over.

No, he's *running* over, it's time to ignite the afterburners.

My ears go back and I fly down the street with Dog hot on my tail— literally! I'm breathing so heavy I think I'm going to pass out.

I am so out of condition! A degree in cat napping on my lounge lookout post isn't going to get me in shape for an unplanned street sprint away from that box with legs.

Around the corner, over the fence—I can't go much further, my lungs are a whisker off from exploding. I make a last ditch run for a tree I spot at a park I've never seen before.

I peg my way up to a branch high enough to give me a clear vantage point. I've lost him. Bandit is nowhere to be seen.

Whew, what a relief! I think. *That was close.*

MAGGIE

By the time I was eight years old, I had found 13 missing car keys, 7 pens, 1 envelope of $100 notes, 3 dogs and 7 cats. Fast forward 30 years and word had hit the street that this cross Ace Ventura Pet Detective/Dr. Dolittle hybrid was doing good things for the missing animal community and my phone started ringing a little too often for my liking.

Finding someone's much loved animal family member kept me going, but of course not all investigations are successful. It was a constant swing between jubilation and devastation. There are many factors involved here; the animal leaving of their own accord, them being stolen and hidden from view, they've passed, they don't want to be found for any number of reasons and even the energy between the animals and their people can make it near impossible to connect with their animal.

I had developed this knack of flying my energy self to the missing animal's location to view the world from their current viewpoint—to see through their eyes, hear through their ears, feel their surroundings and taste and smell what they could taste and smell.

I know that all sounds a bit Hollywood, but there you go, that's what I do. Call it a party trick if that makes you feel safer!

The issue we have today is 3-year-old Winnie the cat who was last seen at home on the lounge 17 days ago. Has she been stolen? Is she at someone's house? Is she trapped? Is she alive? Is she injured? How far from home is she? So many questions.

Understandably, Mum is almost incoherent with panic, guilt and blame for Winnie's vanishing act. The only thing she has found to date is her open window and her cat missing and, reading her email, it crosses my mind that a degree in psychology would be helpful.

To: Maggie Munroe
From: Janice McDonald
Subject: Help! My cat is missing

I'm looking everywhere. I can feel she doesn't feel well. While I'm panicking, I'm doing my best to stay calm. It isn't easy. I don't know what to do, I don't know where else to look. I can't sleep thinking of her out there at night with the coyotes around. Can you please help?"

Janice

Grabbing paper to sit and prepare for this session, I jolt with a vision my team presented me at the 1:30 a.m. meeting: a small box with a square cut hole in the front. Through my mind, I reach out with my energy fingers and tap this box and I can feel it is wooden. As I draw it closer for more detail, I see it is an olive green in colour.

Where is this box? I wonder. And what is the relevance to Winnie?

I hear running water and an angry dog growling.

Animals Speak

Stop! I say in my mind to my deliverers of information.

Children laughing. They sound young.

Wait, team, I think. *I need paper. Can you let me at least sit down?*

My brain is in overdrive as I search for that missing paper someone must have broken in and stolen while I was asleep. I don't want to miss any of this information flurrying in.

This is how it works, you see. It doesn't matter that I have my ritual to prepare for a missing animal; once the booking drops, the visions start flooding the etheric airwaves.

Without missing a beat, I locate the mysteriously stolen paper (that I had hidden under a pile of bills), sit and write like I'm possessed for the next hour. *So much coming in today,* I think to myself. *Let's hope it can bring Winnie home.*

There is a dog very close. I can hear him as if he's underneath me.

I feel like I want to look up. I force myself to look down and my head pops up. *She must be up high,* I think.

Don't overthink it, Maggie, I scold myself, write it all down and then go back and detective it.

> A school bell.
> She's in a confined space.
> Trapped.
> Cannot get herself out, she needs assistance.
> Jackhammers, men yelling, earthmoving equipment.
> Long wild grass.
> Helicopter overhead.

> Running water tastes fresh.
> White dirt road.
> Large, grassed area surrounded by trees.
> BIG tree. Bigger than the rest. It stands out.
> Wooden box, olive green.
> I see Winnie's eyes looking through a gap.
> Icecream van music playing.
> Hamburger smell.
> I hear the words "Look up" on repeat.

Winnie's energy is very, very weak—she's slipping—there's a matter of a few days or even hours to find her now. She's on borrowed time. I feel rushed and I pressure myself to lock onto something substantial, a landmark, a sign, a building, anything that can pin a location.

There's a sign. Rectangle shape with top corners curved, bottom square edged. A pine tree painted in white on the left. There are words I can't read. Is it a single word or two words? I strain trying to see what I can't make out.

Maybe this is enough for Janice to go on. I'm certain Winnie is two, maybe three, blocks from home.

This must get to her before the sun slides, there is so little time and there's an hour of light left. I know she *can* be found; I just don't know if she *will*.

As quickly as I can I sort through my scrawly notes, I fly my fingers across the keyboard and send them over to Janice. I cross every one of my fingers, hoping all roads lead to Winnie. I tell Winnie to hang in there, Mum is looking for her.

WINNIE

Now that the damn dog has disappeared, I notice how high I am up this tree.

Smart one, Winnie, I scowl to myself, *now what are you going to do?*

I check my claws are firmly locked into this branch I'm standing on before looking around for an exit strategy. Yes, a square flat platform on the next branch over. If I can get onto that box Mum should be here soon to retrieve me from this predicament.

Hunkering low to the branch, I scoot across to the wooden ledge and against my better judgment cinch in and squeeze myself through the opening of this box. It was tight and there is barely space to turn around, but I'm a cat and I'm a master at fitting into small hideouts. There is just one problem. And quite a big one, it turns out. I got myself in, but I can't get out!

Day turned into night into day and still no Mum. *What is she waiting for?* I was hungry and tired and I needed her pats and dulcet tones.

Sun up, sun down, sun up ... every day feeling weaker and weaker.

My eyes drift closed, my weakening body pulling me into a deep, deep sleep...

"WINNIE! WIIINNNNIIIEEEE. Where are you, beautiful girl? Show me where you are—it's time to come home."

I hear Mum's voice like a distant memory poking through a fog. It takes my remaining effort to stand and peer through a gap to find myself eyeball to eyeball with a man holding a canvas bag. I was too tired to care that this man might be trouble. I heard Mum's voice and that must mean he's safe.

MAGGIE

I hadn't slept for three days worrying about Winnie, wondering what I'd missed. Maybe there was more to see today that might help, but I couldn't settle to even try to look for her.

What was going on? I wondered. I was edgy and pacing around the house looking for I don't even know what.

Just sit and check in on Winnie and see how she is, I thought. *At least you can do that surely!*

Where's Janice? What's happening? I'd refreshed my email and checked my phone at least 15 times in the last hour and— nothing.

It was 10:30 a.m. and in two hours, I would understand this restlessness.

To: Maggie Munroe
From: Janice McDonald
Subject: Winnie is Home!

Maggie, I can't believe it. I've been crying for the last two hours. We found Winnie. She was literally 2 streets away near the Lensit Elementary School oval. The biggest most beautiful Oak Tree butted up against the school has a bird box hanging halfway up and there she was stuck inside. Silly thing.

There is construction at the school as they're building a performing arts room so all the noises you were hearing are right here. So many things you mentioned helped us locate her. It was like a needle in a haystack and every day that went by the more scared and desperate I became. The bird box was a browny green colour and was so hard to see. It was only that I was walking around the trees looking up and the grounds keeper came and asked me what I was doing. He'd hung the box so he knew what you might have been seeing and took me straight to Winnie.

The thing that sent me to this school was the sign. You mentioned a rectangle sign with a pine tree in white. Well, that's the sign to the school at the driveway which is lined with pine trees.

Did I mention I have been crying? I'm still crying writing this. She's lost a lot of weight and is very dehydrated, but she's in good hands with the Vet now. They want to keep her there for two days. I can't wait to bring her home. 20 days! Can you believe it. I've been a wreck for 20 days. Tonight, I can sleep knowing she is home. Thank you Thank you Thank you. Your work means the world to me.

Love,
Janice

Animals go missing all day every day and it's important to be prepared for the possibility it may happen to you.

The number of animals being stolen is growing by the minute; they are slipping out of that gate or door left ajar and getting themselves lost or they may even leave of their own accord. No one believes that to be a possibility, but if your animals are unhappy with their circumstances at home or if they consider their teachings to their people complete, they will move on.

Make yourself familiar with organisations available in your area that could help you find your missing animal and consider utilising their services should the situation arrive. These are groups like Intuitive Investigators, Pet Detectives and K9 Trackers. For information about how you can work with me in this capacity, see the page on my website for Rommie Buhler — Intuitive Tracking services.

A word on cats.

If you are searching for a lost cat, start close to home and work outwards. They are often closer to home than you may think. They also get into EVERYTHING from washing machines to pool filter enclosures, to ceiling spaces to stormwater drains to bird boxes to garden sheds, under decks, garages, neighbours' boats, construction sites and so many other nooks and crannies. I have seen cats trapped in all these locations.

What I have found is people are happy to place flyers in the mailboxes of their neighbours or even knock on their door, but they are not personally getting into their yards and looking into all possibilities. Your neighbours are not going to look for your pets with the diligence that you would so make sure it is you searching their property (with permission).

BE PREPARED WITH YOUR MISSING ANIMAL'S TOOLBOX
Have all the necessary items in place that you could pull out at a moment's notice.

- *Have individual photos of your animals at the ready for posters, flyers and Facebook pages.*
- *Keep your Microchip address and phone details updated if you have moved house.*
- *If your animal is found and being kept by someone, ensure you have proof of ownership available.*

*For more ideas, see the section on Missing & Stolen Animals at the end of this book.

7

STOP SCRATCHING, AUGUST!

"My little dog—a heartbeat at my feet."
~ Edith Wharton

AUGUST

There's an army of ants having a dance party under my skin and there's not a single maneuver that makes it go away.

I don't know why, but that lady looking after me insists I don't scratch.

"STOP SCRATCHING, AUGUST," she says.

Well, that's easier said than done, isn't it lady!

You've got to ask yourself if that's even a fair thing to ask of a dog! If there's an itch, you've gotta scratch it, don't you?

There's not a day that goes by that I haven't had this prickly feeling. Some days it's so bad my hair tears out and I dig holes in my skin. They're not good days, this constant sensation of having stuck my paw in a power socket makes my innards fizz you know. Well, you probably don't know, but that's what it feels like, this continual humming on my insides.

Kate, my interim Mum, also thinks I smell like an anus.

"August, you stink like a tub of rotting anuses!" she says. "When did you last have a bath?"

I can tell you now, I have smelled plenty of anuses in my life and that, my friends, is my absolute pleasure!

I wonder if that's even a serious question considering I had a bath rolling on a dead bird when she took me for my walk this morning. I would say on a scale of 1-10, 10 smelling like a quality dog's anus, that I would be an 11.

But that's not their version of a bath, is it. It's cold water from the green snake lying on the grass, some feral smelling shampoo and a harsh ruffling up with a sandpaper towel.

And that's where we're at now. Kate's got the snake out, the sandpaper and that off-smelling, foamy business. She even shows it to me like I can read.

"I'm a dog Kate, I can't read!" I say with an eye roll your mother would be proud of.

The noose around my neck is pegging me next to that grass snake's post on the wall. I try pulling away, but I'm locked on and going nowhere.

"August, don't be difficult now. It's time to stop that scratching and this shampoo is going to help you."

Rommie Buhler

How should I act today, I wondered.

Do I hook that tail through the legs and show her I'm about to die? Or do I pull out my psycho dog and try to put her off? I opt for throat cut dog and drill my best eyes that say, *if you follow through with this, I will die and it will be your fault.*

How are you going to explain that to Mum and Dad when they return from their vacay, Kate!

The thing you've gotta remember people is washing us itchy dogs doesn't stop the scratching. And that's the problem we're talking about today because in case I hadn't told you yet, those ant armies are sending me into a tailspin and I'm back to digging sticky trenches in my skin.

"August, it's time we came to an agreement," Kate says. "We have two weeks together and your scratching is going to send me to a mental institution. I can't imagine how John and Cheryl deal with this all day every day. So… I am going to do some research and work this out before I leave. This just cannot be comfortable for you."

You got that right, lady, I think nibbling at my paws.

"Are you in agreeance to anything I do to try to help you out of this predicament you seem to be in?" she asks, staring at me.

I stop mid-lick and look at her suspiciously. I have a list of "depends…" ready to roll off my tongue, but since she hasn't heard any of my previous requests I've made in this last week, there's no point in even thinking she's going to listen to me now.

"Okay then, August," she says, "It's a process of elimination. We are going to start with grass allergies and see what happens."

Animals Speak

I tell Kate, *Mum's already been down that road and it didn't help*, but she must be busy plotting because she's not hearing me. If she asked me, I could tell her what the problem was—but no! No-one listens to what August has to say!

I drag myself outside and find my itch tree. I've told my cat brother Echo about this tree and he uses it too. And that must mean it's good since he doesn't pay attention to anything else I have to say. Anyway, this tree has bark that's rough and knobbly and when you line up those prickly ants and rub vigorously back and forth… *ohhhhh* it makes me go all wobbly at the knees.

The following week is a long one as Kate works through her possible causes and magic potions. None of which helped me one bit, but I knew that, didn't I. I've tried these things before.

There are things that August likes though and it wasn't all bad. I had extra belly rubs while Kate was looking for fleas, *tick* for August. She brushed me every day which is equivalent in knee wobbles to my itch tree, another *tick* for August. My ears were stroked looking for more creatures and that… well think Dalai Dog Llama and you'll know how that feels.

We're not left often and to date we haven't been fussed with some of the house sitters Mum and Dad bring in to look after Echo and me. There was one lady that didn't fill our water bowl up once and it was bone dry when she finally left. I was envisaging the title of our eulogies— *August and Echo die a painful and tragic death because stupid pet sitter didn't fill up their water bowl!* It was just lucky when Mum and Dad came home to save us.

But back to this lady Kate, she's pedantic and a lot too clean, but she must like us because she's determined to sort out my ant troop before she leaves. And I figure if she likes us then I might try and like her too.

Rommie Buhler

Before I get to liking her, I have something to say because she insisted on this yesterday and I was *not* happy.

August does not want his bed cleaned any more than he wants his dead bird deodorant washed off his body. When I dig up my hangi bones and bring them back to my bed, that is where they stay. There are bone remnants housed in that fabric from 1829 and that is a big no to anyone thinking it's the right thing to do to remove those baked fragments.

Kate crossed the line there yesterday and August wasn't happy!

Where was I?

Oh, that's right, I was talking about liking....

"August, I found a new shampoo to try on you and an itch spray", Kate yells from the other end of the house.

Scratch that last comment. Which of you other dogs get washed *twice* in one week? I flop to the ground with a grunt of disdain for what's to come.

Did I already say I know what's wrong with me? Yeah, I'm smart, I know what's going on here. Do you think someone could ask me instead of working through those lists because it's not grass or pollen, it's not mold or shampoo or mange or the sky or fleas or mites or…

"August, I have an idea," Kate says. "I've been looking at what you're eating and I think that needs changing."

Waity waity, my head shoots up with interest! Sherlock Kate is onto something here and I want to go and address her in person.

I find her leaning over the kitchen bench tapping onto a screen fervently reading and writing. *What is she up to?* I wonder. I don't wonder for too long as the troops are back and I need to get them out of here.

It's exhausting this business, you know. Scratching, licking, chewing, scratching, licking, chewing, scratching, licking, chewing, scratching, licking, chewing…

Dad would always tell me how fun I was, but now I spend so much time thinking about how I can stop this feeling that I don't feel very fun at all. In fact, I'm a very miserable August.

"Augie…"

Augie? I stop in my tracks— that's a new one. Getting a bit familiar there aren't you, Kat!

"I'm going to the raw pet store to get you some new food that will hopefully make you feel better," she says. "I'll paraphrase here, Augie, but kibble and processed food is basically like eating junk food every day. It's an easy way to feed you and Echo, but it's empty of nutrition and it's full of preservatives. I'm going to get some for Echo while I'm there. I think we're onto something here, buddy," she says with a smile.

Tell me something I don't know, Kat! My dinner makes me feel sick all of the time, not to mention empty, tired and moody so yes, please get to the raw pet store and sort my bowl's contents out immediately.

Augie (and Echo) were taken off kibble and canned food and started that afternoon on their new raw diet. Within hours, Augie's ant army had reduced to almost nothing, his itch factor had all but stopped, he had energy he never knew he could have and his mood did a 360-about turn. Not that he stopped being sarcastic and argumentative—after all this is *August* we are talking about. A few weeks in and his itchiness was completely gone, the sores had healed, the hair was growing back and he was no longer licking his paws and chewing.

Kate is on the top of the housesitting list when John and Cheryl go away and even though she still insists on baths and bed washing (which August still smarts over) Kat and Augie have become very good friends.

Itchiness can be a complex problem to unravel, but if you can imagine yourself having that itch you can never seem to scratch you would want to dive deep into working it out. Unless your animals are wild, they are completely reliant on you and it is your responsibility to educate yourself in a way that provides them with the greatest of care.

Animals I see that are itchy are very often also hot (too much Yang). They will be the ones looking for shade, cool dirt to lie in, the pool, air conditioning or anywhere they can cool themselves down. A side note here with hot animals: I regularly note they have a red tongue, digestive problems and anxious tendencies. The opposite is true for animals I see that are cold (too much Yin). They will have a pale tongue and cold extremities and it can help feeding them the more warming foods. They will be the ones chasing the warm sun, heaters and warm, cozy blankets. I'm not an expert on Traditional Chinese Veterinary Medicine (TCVM) so I would consult with a Vet who works with TCVM so they can guide you on ways to heal your animals from the *inside out. (*See also: Dr. Judy Morgan in the Resources section at the back of this book.)*

Digestive disorders are one of the biggest problems I see in nearly every cat and dog I speak with. Can you imagine feeling nauseous, under-energised and generally lacklustre all day every day? This is how they feel most of the time and it doesn't have to be that way. Nutrition is such an important part of their overall physical and emotional wellbeing and it is entirely in your hands what goes into their dinner bowl.

There is no 'best way' to feed your animals; they are all uniquely built and have different requirements based on their age, breed, species, etc. but while kibble and highly processed canned food may be convenient and cheap, they are also one of the biggest culprits to so many of the problems people are experiencing with their animals today.

Knowledge is power— take the time to learn as much as you can about nutrition and all that is available to care for your animal/s. If something doesn't work, find another way; keep searching until you find what works.

---

*See also: Hair Mineral Analysis and Bio Compatibility Testing in the 33 Things Our Animals Need Us to Know (Itching, Scratching, Licking and Chewing section) in the back of this book.

8
SCOTTY HAS AN ADDICTION HE CAN'T SHAKE

"Cats leave paw prints in your heart, forever and always."
~ Unknown

THE DAY OF MY FUNERAL

Scotty Stanthorpe was lying face to the sun, eyes closed under the tree fern behind the landing at the side of the house. The lushness of the garden was a stark contrast to how Scotty was feeling in that moment right before he died.

But it was only a contrast from an outsider's perspective looking in. Scotty himself was as ready and calm as a Zen Monk. So ready, in fact, he'd already walked out of his furry house and was sitting watching himself come to his very natural earthly conclusion.

2 YEARS AGO

When I looked up and saw Mum waltz through the front door I started shaking like a sheet in a tornado. You might be waiting for me to tell you I was scared or something, but if there's one thing you'll want to know about me, it's how much food excites my insides and that was exactly what I could see in Mum's clutches.

There is something else you need to know and that is I am loud. I mean how do you expect me to tell everyone I'm about to burst open when there's food incoming. Mum's always telling people I'm no lamp post and I haven't heard a lamp post make noise so I'm guessing she's trying to say I'm noisy. I've noticed that people are funny when they try explaining things. It's like they talk backwards. I might only be a cat, but in my way of thinking, it would straight out be easier if you just said I was loud.

What I know today is I've been yelling for 15 solid minutes and—nothing! Mum has the dawdle on getting that bowl of crunchy cakes into my eating precinct and I could very well die from starvation if she doesn't peg it up a gear.

Plan B: I'm heading in for some twists… 7, 8, 9, 10 weaves in and around her legs and swoop, there I am in her arms on the way to the door.

NO! This is bad news. I'll be forgotten out there, my stomach's completely empty, I'm weak with fatigue and death is imminent.

SCOTTTYYY'S HUNNNGGGRRYYY I yell, twisting and flailing furiously to no avail.

"Too bad Scotty," Mum says, "It's not time yet." She dumps me with what I didn't think was too much consideration for my near-death situation, on my proverbial hairy butt for who knows how long.

How is it that Frederick gets fed two hours earlier than me? I think as I drag my sorry self to the fern hoping I won't pass out before I get there. A flash of yellow catches my side eye and I stop dead in my tracks.

Helloooo! Looky looky here... is that a bag of dog kibbles I see hiding behind that hairy thing on a stick under the stairs?

Mum didn't think that through, did she, I think to myself as I launch all claws and teeth into the side of that belly heaven bag shredding it open for the world to see.

My jaw moves one frenzied crunch after another.

Slow down, Scotty, I say to myself without a second thought to the idea of slowing down.

I'd noticed the pee release was feeling kinda strained lately. Something was up with the pipes and I knew these crackers were the culprit but I couldn't stop myself.

Mum had started calling me crack cat, which to be honest I found quite offensive, but I'm starting to wonder if she might be onto something. The trouble was, the more I tried not to eat the crunch cakes, the more I couldn't stay away. I knew I was in a bit of a pickle with it all.

Collapsing under my favourite fern, I lie there contemplating my kibble crack addiction.

I wake up before I even knew I'd been asleep with a desperate urge to pee.

Squat down low, wait for the juice to get to the end of the pipe aaaaannndddd .... nothing!

Animals Speak

Take a couple of turns and try again.

Nope, nothing, zero, zip, nata. No pee. My head feels hot and that pee bag is swollen to breaking point.

Not good, Scotty, not good, I pant starting to worry. Desperate to pee and nothing's coming out!

So uncomfortably full.

Mum has told me to show her when things are acting up so on this day, I knew it was time to do exactly that. I made sure she was standing in front of the litter box and got positioned into the "no pee" stance. Not only did Mum notice, but she moved like someone lit a rocket under her. We were in the car before I'd even had a chance to flick that sticky litter pellet out of my toe pad.

My heart sinks! I see that door and I knew precisely the hell chamber Mum had brought me to.

Dr. Kennett! My least favourite person and Scotty did not want to be seeing her today. I close my eyes hoping more than anything I'll be transported back to my fern, my refuge.

One minute I've got fingers pushing into my pee balloon, the next I'm waking up in a cage overhearing that crushing conversation with Mum about one of my favourite subjects—food! Mum is asking Dr. Kennett about taking my crack crunchies away and she is whole heartedly agreeing with this arrangement.

Surely, I did not hear that correctly, I think. *The anesthetic hasn't worn off yet. I must be dreaming.*

"Get me out of here this minute, we need to have a talk," I yell through my drugged haze.

Why is no one listening to me? This is a life and death situation and I need to be heard!

Nothing.

After what seems like days too many, I am back home under strict instructions that there will be no Scotty kibbles. I can't believe my pointy ears! What is this nonsense she speaks of. It is fair to say that I was certain I would die by the end of the week.

"Scotty, there are some changes we're going to make to your diet," Mum calls out from the kitchen. "You had crystals blocking your pee pipe and you nearly died. We got you there just in time, Scotty, but if we don't change things, you will be back with Dr. Kennett and neither of us want that."

"And Scotty," she says, "I need to test the pH in your urine every day so I need you to pee in your litter tray so I can test it okay?"

I don't know what any of that meant, but I know I'm not thrilled. I decided I would keep a "Scotty's Food Torture Diary" for one month and if I am unhappy with this arrangement and still alive, I will stage a protest.

DAY 1 OF SCOTTY'S FOOD TORTURE DIARY

No biscuits. Scotty is very unhappy and starving. Could die.

Raw chicken mince and this new stuff Mum calls BARF. Chicken mince is okay. Barf, I will not eat this fur ball puke. Do not be on my plate again.

Raw chicken wing piece. Tasty. These can stay.

DAY 2 OF SCOTTY'S FOOD TORTURE DIARY

No biscuits. Scotty is still unhappy, bordering on angry and almost certain he will die of starvation. There are merely hours left until he dies.

Raw chicken mince. Yes, this is good.

BARF. It smells worse than Frederick's butt and I will not eat anything that smells like dog butt. Refuse to eat, do not feed this to me again. Hunger strike imminent.

Chicken wing. The only thing keeping me alive.

DAY 7 OF SCOTTY'S FOOD TORTURE DIARY

No biscuits. Has not yet died of starvation, but there is still a chance this will happen. Everything is very uncertain.

Raw chicken mince and raw chicken wing. When I leave those wings long enough, they get warm like a bird's body temperature and that's very pleasing. Very happy.

BARF. Still smells like dog butt, but it's not as bad as day one. Still just looking. Eating this is currently under consideration.

DAY 16 OF SCOTTY'S FOOD TORTURE DIARY

No biscuits. Still alive. Uncertain as to how long that will last. Very disappointed in this current arrangement. Still considering hunger strike.

Raw chicken mince and chicken wing. Why aren't those bird wings on my plate every day? First of several upcoming complaints issued.

BARF. Have attempted to eat this medicine food as Mum calls it and it doesn't taste like dog butt. Confused.

DAY 23 OF SCOTTY'S FOOD TORTURE DIARY

No biscuits. Attempted a hunger strike, but I didn't make it past 30 seconds. I'm certain this is a joke and Mum will come to her senses any day now.

Raw chicken mince. No change.

Chicken wings are back. Unhappy with the delay, complaint does not seem to have been heard. Will issue a 3rd and final complaint.

BARF. When mixed in with plain chicken mince I can forget it's there. Mum cried and is seemingly very happy. Have decided that people are definitely weird.

DAY 30 THE LAST DAY OF SCOTTY'S FOOD TORTURE DIARY

No biscuits. Cravings have reduced dramatically and it's possible I may not die. Disappointed that Mum thinks this is funny.

Raw chicken mince. Why is there less on my plate? Let me show you where the bigger spoons are.

Raw wings are a great success to my jaw and stomach recess.

BARF. Can happily eat this mixed with chicken or by itself. Still smells like a dog's butt. Have determined that this is an ace up my sleeve. If I eat what she puts out, then I can manipulate Mum to let me outside for a final night survey of the area before bed.

WRAP UP OF SCOTTY'S 30 DAYS OF FOOD TORTURE

My gizzards feel happy and I'm properly full for the first time ever. I'm not sure I understand this phenomenon with the amount of crack cakes I have savaged to date and never feeling fully filled up. I have more energy than I remember, and I'm not thirsty all the time. I will continue on under Mum's harsh eating regime without assuming I will probably die. Will refrain from hunger strike until further notice.

Signed:
Scotty Stanthorpe

You might think this is the end of my story, but sadly it didn't end all happy crunchy cracks. Another serious blockage a year later and six months on from that, I had a bad case of kidney disease. I denied it, of course, but I did find my head back in Frederick's kibble bag. I couldn't help it! They were calling out to me.

I had my tongue in the shower, the toilet bowl, the sink, the fountain and still, I was thirsty. So very thirsty.

And hot! My body was radiating enough heat to power a small village. Very, very hot.

Now here's the interesting thing that Mum took a while to get a handle on: none of this was new to me. I'd planned it, you see. I had agreed at my pre-earth landing meeting with my Cat Mentors that I would only be with my Mum for a short while. It wouldn't take her long to learn unconditional love, it was my job to make sure of that. And since her earlier cat Stinks had died from kidney disease, she knew what she was looking for, so I decided that would be my way of teaching her this important lesson.

Rommie Buhler

I mean, it wasn't pretty. Is it ever?! Mum and I were a tight pair of cats and humans and she could read me well. She knew how to care for me right to the end too. It got to the stage where I couldn't walk and she knew to carry me to the water bowl, she would lift me outside and we'd sit in the sun together, she would talk to me, brush me and tell me she loved me.

And then it was time for Scotty to go back home. I remember her asking me if I wanted to die in my own garden at home or if I wanted help. I told her I wanted to be under my fern and so that's what I did. We had our last hours together and I went and lay under my home tree, closed my eyes and drifted away from my body.

Hey, hey, hey, before you go and get all moist eyed on me, I'm still here. That's right, I'm here and Mum knows it, she sees me in her mind and she hears my big noisy voice. Ha, I was noisy, that's for sure. Did I love the sound of my voice! Yes, Siree Bob, I did indeed.

But Mum… On that last day, she took it rough. She cried so hard I almost felt I needed to drop back down there for a minute. But we all know that's not how life works so I just sat with her and let her run it out. It took her a long time to put me back into her thoughts. I kept knocking, but she wouldn't answer.

I've told her to let go of me leaving so early in life and to stop kicking herself for me dying of kidney disease. I chose that way because I knew she would see it. It's not her fault so you can't blame yourself can you. But that's what you humans do isn't it, always feeling guilty and blaming yourselves. If you could just see it for what it is and keep learning, that's all. That's all.

Now I'm just telling you this so don't go telling anyone, but guess what's going to happen! That's right, I am going to be back with my Mum before she packs it in. That's right, I will be back and she will know because I will be as loud as I was, I will stick my nose in her eyes and ears like I always did and I will lie under her left armpit when she sleeps just like I did then too.

That's right. Scotty is not gone— he will be back.

> *In the words of one of my Vets, "A female cat's urethra is like a highway; a male cat's urethra is like a thread of cotton". I have had a cat with a blocked urethra die, I have had a cat with a blocked urethra just scrape through death to later die from kidney disease. I have stopped counting the number of clients I have had over the years with the same problem. I will say that most of these cats were male and all with diets of 90% kibble and 10% highly processed canned food —mine included, until the penny finally dropped that I played a big part in this painful and unnecessary health condition and completely changed their nutrition plan.*
>
> *There is absolutely nothing beneficial about kibble. I heard a Vet recently call it evil and I couldn't agree more. I will say this, kibble is detrimental to the feline urinary system and I urge you to drop any beliefs you may have around animal nutrition and do your own thorough and unbiased research on why you must get your cats and dogs off dried food and eating a more species-specific diet. And no, cats are not always easy to transition to raw food eating, but with patience and "being the food boss," it is possible.*
>
> ---
>
> **For more information on Raw Food Eating, see the Resources section at the back of this book.*

9
THE WORST MORNING OF HARLEY'S LIFE

"Animals are born who they are, accept it, and that is that. They live with greater peace than people do."

~ Gregory Maguire

It was still dark but early on the worst morning of my life, one month after Molly died. I remember the vomiting most clearly. Probably because it was preceded by two small "turns" as Dad called them, that made me shake uncontrollably.

Have you ever had that, where your body shakes uncontrollably?

Everything goes a bit weird, your legs do this jerky thing like they have a mind of their own and you can't stop it. This frothy stuff comes out of your mouth and the second time I bit my tongue which hurt a lot when I got back with it again. You sort of lose your sense of everything for a while, but apparently I thrash around some.

I'm one month shy of nine and Dad says I like people. I suppose I do. I mean, if it lands me a scratch behind the ears then I like people very much. What dog do you know that doesn't love ear scratches? Because when you think about it, they're not that easy to get to when you're a dog. He also says I eat everything I can get my mouth around and I'd say that he's probably right there.

You might also want to know my name's Harley. When I was born, Dad announced to anyone that would listen that I was named after Harley Jasper, one of his favourite baseball players and that makes me feel pretty good about myself. Not everyone's named after someone famous. Greatest pitcher of all time he says and that must mean I'm the greatest Staffordshire Bull Terrier of all time.

The problem lately was I'd been feeling a bit wonky. I don't know the right words to describe wonky, but my eyes couldn't see so good and my guts were a bit off. And sweaty. Yeah, that one's a bit obscure, but I sort of feel hot or something. And now I come to think of it, it's like my nostrils are cleaned out on the inside.

Did I tell you already Dad bought us a house? It's got the hugest backyard you've ever seen with all this grass and dirt, and all these rocks and trees. Whoever those people were before us, they had this stinky pit thing where they used to throw food scraps and there are some ripe smells in there. Ripe in a good way. In a way Harley wants to get in and have a roll. I'm pretty sure this is what heaven's going to look like. Not that I'm ready to see what heaven looks like at this point in my short life, but you know what I mean. I'm just talking about how I think this could be it, I don't want to go there yet.

You might notice I talk a lot. That's because I think there's a lot you need to know, but before I was talking about me, I started to tell you about the worst morning of my life. Well, that was one month after Molly died. She was my sister. Not my real life sister, nothing like that. She was a cat so she couldn't be my real sister, could she. But we were a team and she just up and died one day. Dad told

Mum he didn't know what had happened, she just carked it and there she was on the back patio one afternoon.

When you're named after a famous baseball player it might be expected that you're strong and I tried real hard to be stoic Harley, but I just couldn't hold it. Molly was my sleeping buddy. She made me feel safe in the dark. Because if I tell you another truth about me, I'm not that fussed with the dark. I don't know why, but it just doesn't feel right. I was really sad when she left us and I lost all my energy for a while. Mum told Dad that she was afraid I was grieving or something, but it was just that I needed some Harley time.

I got to feeling right about Molly and start feeling wonky and spacey and having these fits. Dad's worried about me and after the first time he took me to see Dr. Pat. Besides high tailing it out of there back home, the only thing I like about Dr. Pat's office are the treats. All those noises and smells and other cats and dogs in there, well they're just downright scary. I get quivery when I'm scared and that doesn't make me feel right at all.

You might not have figured it out, but I can tell you it was good to get home. Dad took me out the back and we did some gardening together. To be perfectly honest I still wasn't feeling too special so I sniffed around a bit before I lay there watching him unload this trailer of dirt. It's not that I wanted to feel this way because when there's a pile of dirt that has Harley treats in there, that needs my thorough attention and investigation.

In that week before I almost died, Dad decided to work from home so he could keep watch over me. He'd take me out to do my business and walk with me around the garden. Smells weren't exciting me like they usually do, but I thought if I checked that soil out it might tell my brain to feel better. It made sense when I thought about it. I fossicked around a bit, chewed some soily treats and then before

I could tell it to stop my back was arching and my legs shook real bad again. When it finished, I couldn't walk straight. Everything was out of pitch and I didn't feel right.

I didn't feel good in my body and I didn't feel good when Dad had me back to Dr. Pat's office. He tried testing for more things and we were sent home with some of those horrible tablets that are supposed to take the pain away. I could tell you already they weren't going to work. Remember we had those before and they didn't help. And not only that, they make me feel even worse than I do without them. If something's going to make you feel worse then it's pretty obvious you shouldn't really have it.

I was generally an active dog and that was a bit peculiar because I didn't feel like doing anything or being with anyone. You know when someone doesn't do what they normally do and you know they're not right. That was me. Do you remember me telling you how I didn't like the dark? Well, that's exactly where I wanted to be and I'd found a shaded fort in the spare room under the bed. It was quiet and cool and dark. I figured that if I lay there long enough the old Harley might reappear.

That room had a curious smell. I don't know if it was a bad smell, just an unusual one I hadn't come across before.

I could hear Dad calling me for that horse tablet. If I closed my eyes and pretended I was invisible he might forget.

Or not, as it were.

"Harley."

"Harley, come on boy it's time for your medication. It's going to make you feel better so get yourself out of there."

Dad, that tablet the size of your fist is not making me feel better. Nope. I'm staying right here.

He doesn't seem to hear me as the octopus arms have a hold and are pulling me out.

Oh dear, here it comes again…

Where am I? So disoriented. The more I try to stand up the more I'm falling over. This is a good one this time. And I don't mean good as in *nice* good, I mean good as in *big*. I black out and don't remember a thing. A full body seizure they told me afterwards while we were driving to a new Vet to do yet some more tests.

I've noticed I'm feeling weaker and stranger after every turn and I think Mum's figured that out too because I heard her on the phone to someone that does something with your energy. To be honest I don't even know what that means, but she's had someone out here doing that before and it makes me feel peaceful Harley. That lady is coming after we get back from my brain scan. And then the day after that, there's this man going to have a look at my bones. I wasn't certain if I was happy about any of this poking around, the Vet had done plenty of that the last few days, but I trusted Mum so I said to her that would be okay. Not that she heard me say it was okay, she just went and did it anyway.

Scans and tests and drips and tablets and there was no improvement and still no one knew what to do with me. The bone man found a problem with my shoulder and that made me yelp real loud. While Dad was worried about that, he said it was the most noise I'd made for a week. I don't know if that was a good thing since it hurt more than anything.

Those turns were daily now and it was getting harder to stand back up after each one. And that's when Molly came to talk to me. You know I told you she right rolled over and died and I was sad and all. Well, the thing was I hadn't seen her since and I thought she would have come and visited. Since I was her brother, I expected she should have done that. Well, there I was lying down, because that's all I could do these days, and there she was sitting right in front of me. I thought I was in some kind of dream or something. I asked her where she'd been and she told me she'd been busy doing other things up there with the cat heaven teachers. She said she couldn't stay because she had to get back, but she wanted to tell me that if I wanted to come and live with her I could. And then she just disappeared.

Right then, I had the biggest turn yet. I wondered how I was going to make it through this one, but since I was mostly unconscious, I didn't really need to worry about that. Dad said I had two turns in that one and he was really worried. He had Dr. Pat on standby and we were about to go when I started vomiting. It's not like I haven't vomited before, it's a regular thing for us dogs, but this was violent and I thought right then and there my insides were going to shoot out my mouth and there'd be nothing left.

The only thing I remember after that point was waking up with two wet faces in my face staring at me— Mum and Dad—and they were right out crying their heads off. Harley, well he's not one for crying, but if I wasn't so weak, I might have just joined in.

When my body said it was all right to feel things, I noticed something was different, like a weak version of the old Harley had rolled back into business.

I'd been out cold at Dr. Pats for five days and today I'd come home.

Oh, was it good to be home.

Rommie Buhler

I was real tired still, but when I could stay awake long enough I heard Mum talking about this lady she'd seen that had been talking to me while I was out of it. I mean how's that. You can talk to someone when they're in a long sleep. Well apparently, I told her about the funny smells under the bed and it went from there. Dad had put in new carpet that was poisonous, he was also spraying this weed killer on the lawn, the outside of our house was being painted and that dirt full of Harley treats had toxin stuff in it that wrecked my insides.

I knew my nose felt clean inside, and you know us dogs have their noses close to the ground sniffing everything, well there was so many deadly things going on that my body couldn't handle and it poofed out of service. But not *out* out—not in a way I had to live with Molly again and that was important because, after all, I was only 9 and my job was to help Dad with that big yard. There was no way he could handle all that by himself.

I can say out loud that Harley has prevailed and gets to live another day and any day that's a Harley day is a good day!

When was the last time you thought about the chemicals you use in and around the house and how that might affect your animals? When was the last time you took your dog to the local hiking trail and they'd been spraying toxic pesticides? When was the last time you took your dog to the park or your neighbour's house where they'd been spraying glyphosate?

Toxic chemicals can kill your animals and it is not pretty. I have so many clients I can't list them all but knowing animals that have their noses close to the ground sniff their way around their environment, this is a recipe for disaster. Weed killers I see all the time and have seen clients with itching, listlessness, digestive disorders, seizures and death. I have had a dog poo under a bed every day for three weeks until Mum asked me what was going on. There were two problems here: new carpets had been laid and underneath the mattress was covered in mould. This was an anxious dog that went under this bed as their safety hideout. It started with looking "out of sorts" progressing quickly to the nearest Emergency Vet. He made it through and is still here to tell his story fortunately. This is not a one off; new flooring, toxicity from tiling, new curtains, bleaches and cleaning products, weed killers, paint are regular problems I encounter.

Consider changing to a low tox natural lifestyle and get rid of all chemicals in and around your house. And if you're on good terms with your neighbours, suggest they do the same. If there is poisonous activity going on in your neighbourhood, parks and ovals, keep your animals away.

---

*For more information, see the section on Chemicals in 33 Things Your Animals Need Us to Know in the back of this book.

10

THE RUSTLERS PUT A HOLE IN MY HEART AS BIG AS THE GRAND CANYON

"Don't cry because it's over. Smile because it happened."
~ Ted Geisel

When I was 10, I got a horse that—according to Mr. Brown—no-one else wanted.

I don't know if that's a good or bad thing because if no-one else wanted the horse, what did that say about me? I didn't worry about that for long because when Sawdust came off the trailer, I knew that I didn't need to worry about that anymore.

When he looked in my eye and I looked in his eye, I'd already forgotten that I wondered if that was a good or bad thing that no-one else wanted him. And when we finished looking in each other's eyes it just kind of came to me to call him Sawdust. I suppose it was because he was the colour of that sawdust down at the mill Dad worked at. I'm pretty sure he liked his name because when I asked him if that would be all right, he looked at me and nodded his head.

Now it's not that everything was smooth sailing; he'd had a lot of homes under his belt before he got to me and I could tell he was scared. Mr. Brown said he was a 3-year-old Mustang and he'd so far lived in 11 homes. That's a lot of homes. I'm 10 and I've only lived in one so I can't imagine what it's like to live in 11.

Mr. Brown also said everyone wanted him to do dressage, but he was useless at it and they'd send him away again. I think that's pretty unfair to think he's useless when maybe he didn't even want to do dressage. Just because you're not good at something doesn't mean you're useless. That's like the other boys at school telling me I'm hopeless at football when I don't like football. I don't like football so I certainly don't want to be good at it.

Maybe that's why me and Sawdust got to being such good friends— we both had the same problem with people not understanding us.

I'd never had a horse before and I don't really know why I wanted one so bad, but I knew I just did. Every week I'd ask Dad if I could have a horse and every week he'd say, "No, Son, you can't have a horse".

He also told me I wouldn't look after it because in his mind I don't look after anything, but since I've only broken one thing and that wasn't really my fault, I don't know how he can know already that I won't look after a horse when I haven't actually got a horse.

And by the way, that one thing I broke was a dinner plate that dropped from my hands when Razor, that firecracker of a cat, jumped on the back of my head and bit me. You can't blame me for that when you've got a cat biting your head. Old people are confusing sometimes; they say things like that that don't make any sense.

So, when Mr. Brown dropped off Sawdust I was pretty certain Dad would tell him to come pick him up and take him to his 12th home. When Dad came home from the mill that day, he said he had already spoken to Mr. Brown and they'd arranged for me to keep Sawdust for a month to see if it would work.

I was so excited that I whooped and jumped and yelled, but there's something you've got to know about my Dad—he doesn't much like noise or showing how you feel about things even if they make you excited so he told me to settle down and be quiet. I think he was secretly happy to see me so happy because he brought home this book about how to look after horses.

That night I went to bed early so I could read every page twice before I went to sleep. I'd made a silent pact with Sawdust that this was going to be his last home. I had a month to prove that I could look after him and we needed to get started on being good friends real quick so as quiet as I could I got changed, grabbed the torch I kept under my bed and went out to talk to him.

When I walked into his stall, I said to him the first thing we needed to do was trust each other. The book had said that the rider should be kind to their horses and show them respect to gain their trust so that's what I was going to do. To be honest I wasn't certain what that meant because that made it sound like you had to be something you weren't already. Mum had always told me that I was a kind boy and now I was confused because did that mean I needed to be kinder. That was before she died and now she's not here I can't ask her if I needed to be different.

So, I said to Sawdust that I didn't really know if I had the kindness they talked about in the book and that he'd have to help me. We talked all the time, me and Sawdust. I'd tell him what I thought we were supposed to do and he would show me if I wasn't doing it right.

Every day, Sawdust and I became better friends and he would follow me everywhere like our old dog Leonard used to do when he was alive. When I wasn't at school, which I wish was all the time since I wasn't much into school, I was with Sawdust. He was a friendly horse too. Once I told him he was my horse and I read him our book about being kind and trusting each other, he sort of just stopped being scared. People loved Sawdust. Our house was on a main road and he'd wander down to the fence line and let them come and pat him and feed him carrots.

Another thing about Sawdust, he was real funny. When I was thinking about something that wasn't horses, he would come up behind me and nibble the back of my neck. Now I don't know if you've had horse lips at the back of your neck before, but it's ticklish.

Sawdust was clever too. He'd taught himself to flip the latch off his gate and get out. Dad wouldn't have been happy about that, but he never seemed to do it when he was around. The first time I knew about it, he came over to my bedroom window and stuck his head inside. Dad asked me why I dragged my bed under the window and I told him it was easier to read which it wasn't; I just said that so he wouldn't make me put it back.

That day when Mr. Brown came down to talk to Dad and see how it was going, I think I'd forgotten how to breathe. I felt coiled up like a spring waiting to hear that Sawdust was really, *really* mine to keep. I don't know what it is with adults, but they seem to have a lot to talk about that's not important. For seven whole minutes I had to hear about how Mrs Cunningham in the next two towns over from ours had baked four tea cakes for the school fete. I mean who wants to hear about that when someone's life is on the line.

Finally, they got to Sawdust and me and that's when I realised I had been holding my breath all that time because when Dad said he could stay I nearly fainted. I wrapped my arms around Dad's waist, which he told me to stop doing because I don't know why, but I was so happy that it just came out of me.

Then I realised I hadn't told Sawdust and he was the most important one to tell. I explained to him the whole conversation, including how long it took to talk about Mrs. Cunningham's tea cakes and told him he was in his forever home. I knew he understood because he came right over and put his head over my shoulder and pulled me into his neck. That bit made me cry even though I'm not one for crying.

Sawdust and I had been best friends for six years. That was six years until that day he went missing. We didn't have a big place and I could see most of it from my bedroom window, but when I couldn't see him, I ran to every corner like I might have missed something. Even Dad came to help look for him and he never came to talk to Sawdust.

I was so caught up tight in my chest I thought I might faint like I almost did that other day when Dad said I could keep Sawdust. The police came out and they said they found trailer tracks at the front gate and thought Sawdust had probably been stolen. There were rustlers out there taking horses that weren't theirs and selling them off. I didn't understand why anyone would do that, but apparently 17 had been taken in the last month and they hadn't found any of them. They said they'd do the best they could and let us know if they heard anything.

Animals Speak

One day they told my Dad to ask me to stop ringing them so much, but I didn't listen. It's not their horse that had been stolen. I rang them three times a day for six months. My best friend was missing and my chest had a hole in it as wide as the Grand Canyon.

That next year, I was in a daze. Sometimes I would go to school, but I don't remember anything. I didn't pay attention in class or do any homework. The Headmaster called Dad in one day to talk to him about my grades dropping so low there almost wasn't another grade to go to. I just nodded and mumbled I'd do better whenever he tried to talk to me about it.

Every night, I would stare out my window waiting for him to come around the corner. I was sleeping in his stall for a while until Dad said I couldn't do that. He said that life wasn't always easy and I needed to get over it like he had with Mum when she died. I didn't know what get over it meant—all I knew was my heart had been cut out of my chest and run over by that rustler's trailer.

No one understood why I cared so much about a horse, but they obviously don't know what it's like to have your best friend of six years vanish into thin air. The police said they found the men that took him, but they couldn't tell them where Sawdust had gone. Apparently, they spoke to these men for two days and couldn't prove anything so let them off.

What do you do when there are no answers and no one's ever going to give you any? Every day I want to know where he is, if he's still alive, if he's happy and every day I don't know anything.

Dad brought home this book from a lady he'd met. I suppose she was his girlfriend. I don't know if I liked her, but he said I had to get over that too. He also told me he didn't know what to do with me. I don't know how I felt about that because I didn't know what to do with me either.

This book was called *Grief That Haunts*. Now I don't know about you, but that doesn't sound like the type of book I wanted to read, but I didn't really know what to do with those pieces of Sawdust I'd hidden away to think about another day and Dad said I needed to read it. It was a book I thought Sawdust might need to hear too, wherever he was, so I took it out to his stall and read it out loud so he could hear too.

The lady said it was time to let go, but you could still have hope. I asked Sawdust if we could do that and I could see him nod his head. It didn't mean I was going to forget him; I would never forget Sawdust, but I could remember him without my heart falling on the ground.

I wrote him a letter telling him he was the best friend I'd ever had and that included my best friend at school Joey. I wrote how much I missed him every single day and would remember him forever and that I hoped he'd met another nice horse that he could be with. I gathered up his saddle and blanket and asked Dad if I could put that box he'd made me from the off cuts from the mill in my bedroom. He thought that was odd, but he carried Sawdust's wooden box with his tack and my letter in it to sit under the window.

Not a day goes by that I don't think about Sawdust and remember what we did together and even though everyone wanted me to get over it that just didn't feel right to do that, but I suppose I've just learnt to get on with it.

In my early twenties my cat was stolen from my backyard. His name was Selby and I loved him more than anything in the world. I was absolutely devastated that I couldn't find him and with no traction in my search for him, I packed his food bowl and collar into a bag and found the nearest psychic for help. She was more interested in talking to me about my libido than my missing cat, which was not exactly what I had in mind! It's interesting that 30 years later I am now working as an Intuitive Investigator looking for missing animals. It took me a very long time to move past that raw grief and still now when I think about this, I feel a lot of guilt that I failed him.

Thousands of animals are going missing every day, many of which are not found and the grief that surrounds this is immeasurable. Many of my clients that have had animals that have passed too early or in tragic circumstances or have been stolen or lost and not returned have so much trouble moving beyond this grief, guilt and blame.

One thing I know from speaking with animals in spirit is they never blame their person for the part they think they played in them passing or going missing. On most occasions this is part of their plan prior to coming to earth and what they want from us is to not just see the bigger picture of what life is about but find ways to remember them with love and not trauma. Creating a memory board of photos, writing them a letter, drawing their picture or having an artist draw that for you and having a ceremony can help. Working with a Pet Loss and Grief Specialist to help you through this difficult period can also be extremely beneficial.

---

*For more information on grieving a pet, see the Resources section at the end of this book.

11
33 THINGS OUR ANIMALS NEED US TO KNOW

*"When you truly recognize that animals 'feel',
you will show them greater love and respect."*

~ Rommie Buhler

The following is a selection of the more common client problems that I have encountered over the years. It is difficult to know when to stop this list as the more I try to wind it up, the more I think of what I can include. Amongst other things, 33 represents inspiration and courage—the two things I have drawn on to write this book—so following is a list of *33 Things Our Animals Need Us To Know*.

It is not an A-Z compendium of all animal concerns nor will some of these suggestions be of help to your animals as I'm sure you are aware that health is never a one size fits all solution. This is merely a collection of suggestions to regular questions and problems I am asked about.

You may discover there are no solutions for your particular problem or these offerings do not work for you. My hope is that you will be inspired to know there are many options available to heal and support your animals, perhaps more than you have ever thought possible and I encourage you to never stop searching for answers to your animals' health concerns; they need that from you. Know that in some instances you may need to manage a problem that simply cannot (or is not meant to) be fixed.

On that note, it is worth mentioning that animals have their own life path—pre-planned time on earth before they return to spirit and most often the way they pass has already been planned. There are times when it is not your job to intervene in an animal's journey and nothing you do will return your pet or animal to good health. You may take comfort in the fact that I have never met an animal that has blamed their person for what happens to them; they have a pragmatic, "it is always as it should be", view on death and know that it is a part of life, not the end of life.

In this list I share my thoughts and in certain instances possible reasons, solutions and any helpful tips I think worthy of sharing. I come across many people that have limited income available to spend on specialty services and one I wouldn't ignore is professional veterinary care. In my view this is an essential part of their care so ensure you align yourself with a veterinarian you know and trust. My preference is a Holistic Veterinary approach and depending on their training they offer many of these services as a part of their practice. Many of the touch techniques I mention you can easily learn and cost you nothing but time, commitment and on occasion a dash of patience.

33 THING OUR ANIMALS NEED US TO KNOW

1. ANAL GLANDS IN CATS AND DOGS 105
2. ANIMALS TRAVELLING IN VEHICLES 107
3. ANXIETY 108
4. CATS ARE BORED 112
5. CATS SPRAYING 113
6. CHEMICALS 114
7. CRUCIATE LIGAMENTS IN DOGS 118
8. DEATH, DYING AND GRIEF 120
9. DEHYDRATION 122
10. DEPRESSION & SADNESS 124
11. ELDERLY ANIMALS 126
12. EXCESSIVE BARKING 128
13. FEEDING 129
14. GROOMING AND BRUSHING 131

15. HOLIDAYING WITHOUT YOUR PETS 132

16. HORSE BITS.. 133

17. HORSES MISBEHAVING 134

18. INAPPROPRIATE TOILET HABITS 135

19. ITCHING, SCRATCHING, LICKING AND
    CHEWING DOGS.. 137

20. MIRRORING BEHAVIOUR 141

21. MISSING & STOLEN ANIMALS...................................... 142

22. NAIL TRIMMING... 145

23. NAMING ANIMALS 146

24. PAIN 147

25. PAW PAD BURNS | HEAT & COLD 150

26. POO ABNORMALITIES IN CATS AND DOGS 153

27. PURCHASING ANIMALS.. 156

28. SADDLE FIT.. 157

29. STATIC SHOCK.. 158

30. SUNBURN 159

31. TALKING TO ANIMALS FOR BETTER BEHAVIOUR .. 160

32. VOMITING 163

33. WHISKER STRESS IN CATS & DOGS............................ 165

ANAL GLANDS IN CATS AND DOGS

Getting to know your dog and cats rear end can save you potential surgery!

Dogs

If you've had a dog scoot along your freshly shampooed carpet or grass on their butt, they may need their anal glands tended to. As a general, dogs are able to express their anal glands on their own, but on occasion, that fishy smelling secretion may not empty properly and complications like blockages, infections and abscesses can occur; none of which is comfortable and if left surgery may be required.

All dogs have their own unique make up physically and emotionally and while yours may never need their anal glands cleared, they may need a regular emptying session, or may just need occasional attention. It's always a good idea to have a regular inspection of their rear end so you know.

Keep a look out for:

- Dragging their butt along the floor or grass.
- Extra licking and scratching attention in the anal area.
- Bloody poo.
- Straining or difficulty pooing.
- Fishy odour.
- Swollen and red anus.

Cats

While we may already know all this about our dogs' anal sacs, we may be less familiar with cats. This is their scent-marking juice and will mostly express naturally when doing their poo business, but like our dogs, blockages can occur and stop this fluid releasing. This can be extremely painful and can lead to further infections.

Similar to dogs, notice if your cat is doing any scooting along the ground or excessive licking. These behaviours and redness can be a notification to perform a butt check. Cats hide their pain well and may put up with this discomfort so it's not always easy to spot when something is "off".

A regular anal gland expression is usually a quick and simple procedure at your local Vet. Keep an eye on it so it doesn't become a more difficult problem.

Is it time to get more familiar with your dog's and cat's anus?

ANIMALS TRAVELLING IN VEHICLES

My Thoughts
- Have you ever driven alongside a car with a dog hanging so far out the window you hold your breath hoping they don't fall? Let me tell you, they do fall and jump out of car windows. Make sure you have them harnessed and securely fastened inside the vehicle. Keep the harness short and windows partially lowered.
- Harnessing animals into vehicles may save their life when in a car accident. (And sometimes yours too, as they become a missile if they are not locked in).
- Always consider their welfare and the weather when you are transporting your animals in open backed utes and trucks. Sunburn, burnt feet, dehydration, heat exhaustion, cold, and hyperthermia can and do happen. And make sure they're secure and can't fall or jump off/out.
- If you are transporting your animals in cages on the back of your ute or truck and they are exposed to the elements, ensure cages have appropriate covers.
- Animals can go missing very easily if a door is opened and they're not locked into a transport carrier or secured harness. They can not only be injured or killed in traffic; it can also be very difficult to find them if they get themselves lost. *(*For more on this, see Missing & Stolen Animals.)*

ANXIETY

My Thoughts

This is the most prevalent of all problems I see in my business. While that may partly be the clientele I attract, it is an extremely common issue amongst all animals.

I have spent time intuiting what anxiety looked like in dogs before this modern-day chaos and it is a very different view to what it is now. The anxiety of times past is what I'd call an *instinctual anxiety*—one where they lived in a state of hypervigilance of "who's behind me", "what's around the next corner", etc. My digestive system feels shaky in a way that I am prey, not predator. You could almost say this isn't anxiety at all but rather a state of being acutely (intuitively) aware and alert of their surroundings.

While that is more instinctual, modern-day anxiety I would call a *manmade anxiety* and it has a distinctly different feel to it. While my innards are still shaking, it feels more childlike and "please save me I feel unsafe" and less innate. I am shown this to be anxiety created by people, children, environment and nutrition.

Anxiety can be a complex problem that may need more than one course of care, but there are many options available to start out with. Whatever you choose to do, don't expect an overnight or quick fix; be consistent and commit to the process. If you don't find any of these approaches help your animal, I hope this opens your mind to the possibility to keep searching for a solution.

Are you familiar with what anxiety looks like in your animal? Anxiety can cause many problems with your animal's health and you don't want to miss the signs. Below is a list of some of the signs to look out for.

Dogs and Cats
- Restlessness.
- Peeing/Pooing inside the house.
- Aggression.
- Lip Licking.
- Drooling or salivating.
- Panting.
- Depression.
- Excessive barking or vocalisation/meowing in cats that may sound like they're in distress.
- Yawning.
- Destructive digging or behaviours.
- Pacing.
- Repetitive or compulsive behaviors.
- Excessive grooming.
- Hiding.
- Trembling/shaking.
- Not eating.
- Change in activity levels.

Horses
- Grinding teeth.
- Fidgeting and restless.
- Stillness (not to be confused with calmness).
- Flighty and easily spooked.
- Sweating.
- Excessive chewing.
- Diarrhoea.

- Gastric ulcers.
- Bolting.
- Rearing.
- Weight loss.
- Slower blink rate (increased eye twitch).

Sidenote: On numerous occasions I have found plug-ins designed to help calm animals actually cause them to feel uneasy and often unwell. Observe any changes in their behaviour and remove if there are adverse emotional or physical reactions. If you have multiple animals in your home, know this can affect all of them in some way. Stay aware.

Possible Reasons Behind Anxiety
- Abandonment or rejection.
- Anxious mother's emotional state being transferred in the womb.
- Nutrition.
- Loud noises.
- Separation or being left alone.
- Mistreatment or abuse.
- New people.
- Rehoming.
- Travelling.
- Aging.
- Constant itching.
- Plug-in calming devices.
- Unusual or hot surfaces underfoot.
- Musculoskeletal malalignment.
- Illness.
- Chemicals and toxins.
- Whisker Stress. (*See Whisker Stress.)

Tips and Suggestions
- Emotional Freedom Technique (EFT). *(*See Resources).*
- Specifically composed music. *(*See Pet Acoustics in Resources).*
- Tellington T. Touch. *(*See Resources).*
- Energy Healing including Shamanic Healing and Reiki for animals.
- Emotion Code. *(*See Resources).*
- Homeopathy.
- Flower Essences.
- Correct Nutrition. *(*See Resources).*
- Acupuncture/Acupressure.
- Traditional Chinese Veterinary Medicine.
- Crystals.
- Jin Shin Jyutsu. *(*See Resources)*
- Dog training.
- Chiropractic, Osteopathy and Body Work.
- Animal CBD Oil.
- Hemp Chews.
- Copaiba Oil for Pets.
- Chakra Balancing (including the 8th Brachial "Bonding" Chakra).
- Bioscalar Wave.
- Body wraps.
- Depending on the degree of anxiety, medication may be required as an interim measure.
- Create a low toxin environment.

CATS ARE BORED

My Thoughts

We might think cats are happy to sleep all day, but when you consider their make-up, they are designed to hunt, chase and catch. They are also designed to move. That means they need mental and physical stimulation. If your cat is an outdoor cat, they have a greater chance of being stimulated. Indoor cats need to be played with so have toys that can stimulate their senses and replicate their desire to chase and hunt. This can also help to keep your cat's weight down. If you hear your cat land heavily when they jump down from something, they may be carrying a few too many pounds!

Tips and Suggestions
- Play with your cats at least half an hour a day.
- Have toys available for them that replicate hunting.
- In some instances, you may have to teach your cat to play so if they appear disinterested, persevere as their natural instinct is to chase and hunt.
- Have a bench, lounge, scratching post near a window that they can look out of. If there are trees near the window, hang a bird feeder so there is movement for them to view. While watching birds outside is entertaining their senses, fish tanks can also be their indoor version of Netflix.
- Leave that window open so they get to experience fresh air and all the outside smells.

CATS SPRAYING

My Thoughts
The scent profile of a cat's environment is extremely important. They will rub on visitors, furniture and their owners, etc to leave them with a natural pheromone. When this is disrupted, your cat can start spraying—this is where they are standing with tail vertical and bursts of urine squirt out.

Possible Reasons
- Inside the House:
  - All scent profiles have been cleaned due to spring cleaning.
  - Moving house.
  - Lots of visitors.
  - A new pet coming into the home.
  - Rearranging and redecorating.
  - Stress.
- Outside the House:
  - If their core area has been breached by an intruding cat.
  - When they feel threatened.

Tips and Suggestions
- Educate yourself on cat territories and behaviour.
- Notice if other animals are coming into their area.
- Find an Animal Communicator to understand why they're doing this (*For information on how to work with me, see Find Rommie Buhler Online*).

CHEMICALS

My Thoughts

All animals have their own levels of tolerance, but chemicals at the least can cause skin irritation to the other end of the spectrum where they can be fatal. We have the choice as to what chemicals we use inside and outside our homes, and as you are responsible for your animal's welfare, it is imperative you are aware of where and what you are using and how they are being stored. It is a good question to ask yourself why you're using toxic chemicals and if there is an alternative. Creating a low toxic lifestyle is a healthier option for everyone in the house including yourself.

The list is endless but make yourself familiar with what you have inside or outside the house and what the council or shire is using in local parks or bushland in your area. I can't tell you how many cats and dogs I have consulted with that are being severely affected by weed killers, new carpets and flooring in their homes.

- Laundry detergent and fabric softener.
- Dishwashing detergent and dishwasher tablets that come into contact with food, water bowls, toys, etc.
- Paint, internal and external. This includes what is happening over at neighbouring properties.
- Flooring—carpets, linoleum, rugs and mats.
- Floor cleaners and waxes.
- Tile, grout and grout sealants.
- Snail pellets and rat baits.
- Shampoos, powders, soaps and skin lotions.
- Human bedding material, blankets and pillows.
- Human medications ingested or topically applied.

- Household chemicals and bleach.
- Pesticides indoors and outdoors. This includes the poisons used by your neighbours, local parks and wooded areas where you may be visiting.
- Carpet cleaning chemicals.
- Candles, air fresheners, plug-ins and toilet fresheners.
- Chemicals used to dry clean clothes.
- Cigarette, pipe and cigar smoke.
- Pool chlorine in and out of water.
- Dust mites, mould and pollen.
- Pet food and food packaging (kibble and canned food is particularly a problem).
- Tick and flea control products.
- Dog bowls, especially plastic.
- Dog collars, harnesses, leashes.
- Toys, grooming tools, crates, clothing.
- Plastics—all forms.
- All genetically modified substances.
- Human food ingested.
- Wheat and/or gluten, soy, corn, dairy.
- Some vitamins and supplements.
- Certain aromatherapy oils.
- Sugar and carbohydrates.
- Medications, vaccines, dental work, surgeries, anaesthesia, instruments, all materials used before, during and afterwards.

Tips and Suggestions
Both **Hair Mineral Analysis Testing** and **Bio Compatibility Hair Testing** can be helpful in getting your animal's health back on track. Not all tests are available to all animals, so check around to see if you can find someone that does testing on your particular animal. Some do only cats and dogs, some horses and dogs, some anything from sheep to camels to dogs, cats, horses. It is very simple and painless as you are cutting hair off your animal and sending it off to a lab.

HAIR MINERAL ANALYSIS TESTING
When animals are exposed to toxic heavy metals, they can suffer and become sick. Animals are exposed to all sorts of heavy metals in their everyday environment from their food, drinking water, when they drink water from ponds, dams, creeks, their containers, insecticides, medication, shampoos, etc.

If your animal has:
- Unusual behaviours like eating dirt or debarking trees
- Flaky skin
- Tooth decay
- A rough coat

this can indicate mineral imbalances that can long term lead to disease and ill health.

A **Hair Mineral Analysis Test** will determine what is missing from your animal's diet, including mineral deficiencies and toxicities. It will also detect levels of heavy metals in their body to ultimately encourage better health, prevent disease, cancers and premature aging.

BIO COMPATIBILITY HAIR TESTING

This is a test that tests the compatibility of items and your animal. Again, check around, as there are places that will test 200 items, there are others that will test more like 600.

When your animal has digestive disorders, itchy skin, rashes, allergies, inflammation, arthritis and behavioural problems it is worth investigating this compatibility test where they check compatibility on anything from food, shampoos, medications, bedding, grasses, oils, supplements, cigarette smoke, dust mite, mosquitoes, tennis balls, fleas and much more.

CRUCIATE LIGAMENTS IN DOGS

My Thoughts

Cruciate ligaments are two fibrous bands located within the knee joint that help to keep it stable. When a partial or full ligament tear occurs, this causes not only instability and lameness, but it is also extremely painful for them and may require surgery. It is a very common injury and one I see often. Cruciate tears occur often through landing badly, sudden and awkward twisting and turning, chasing and playing on soft beach sand, carrying too much weight making the joint more susceptible to injury and genetic disorders or inherent weaknesses.

It may be that I live near the beach, or I just draw in these clients, but cruciate tears from playing in soft beach sand is becoming more and more prevalent. At all costs you want to avoid a painful injury and surgery. **Prevention is always better than surgery**. Be the intelligent leader and show them better options, stick with the hard sand.

Tips and Suggestions
- Do not let them play in the soft sand.
- Let them run on the harder, more compacted sand.
- Keep their weight under control. Feed them a nutritious diet and serve the correct quantity to maintain a healthy weight.
- Avoid jumping down from heights and running or slipping downstairs.
- Healing/Rehabilitation Options:
  - Animal Chiropractic Specialists.
  - Animal Osteopath.

- Shamanic Healing.
- Energy Healing.
- Acupuncture.
- If surgery is required, including things like energy healing, acupuncture, magnetic blankets, a specialist in dog chiropractic and consulting with your Holistic Vet for pre- and post-surgery preparation will be of great benefit.

DEATH, DYING AND GRIEF

Death and Dying

Animals understand death (and life) far better than we do. In my many conversations with animals coming to pass and already passed, I know they see death as a part of their journey. It is not the end, but purely a shift in energetic state— one they understand, accept and fully embrace.

What I have been shown on many occasions is when they return to spirit, they rest for a period of time and spend time integrating healing from their teachers and mentors before they go into what I hear is called "camp". Camp can take many years before they go back into a holding pattern for their next pre-birth planning session and return.

At camp, they are separated into sections with other animals where they are able to spend time as that specific animal to decide how they feel about living this type of life in the future. I had a cat client who was 5 years into an 8-year stint in camp and she loved the energy of being the Squirrel. She had tried out being the Cow which she felt was too steady and grounded and the Alligator who she did not like at all and had to negotiate with her mentors to "get out" of that experience as soon as possible. She will be coming back as a squirrel when the time is right.

If we can understand the true nature of life and death, it may be possible for us to live with less guilt and sadness as our animals pass.

Our Grief

It can be traumatic when our pets pass away or are lost or stolen— particularly when we are not expecting it or when a situation like a stolen animal is not returned and is left unresolved. This can leave us with a sense of haunting that is difficult to move past. At some point it is necessary to let go and as a part of this process it may be helpful to seek help from a pet loss and grief specialist (*See Resources*), have a ceremony honouring your pet, write them a letter or journal about what comes up for you when you consider your time shared together or even creating a photo board of memories.

What I have found with all animals I have spoken to that are about to pass or have passed already, they never blame their people for anything that we may blame ourselves for or feel guilty about. Not one animal have I come across has this mindset. It is also important to remember that animals are here living their own life journey and if that is to pass at a certain time or in a particular way that is how it will be and there is not a lot we can do about that. They don't want us to live in grief, to hold off on bringing another animal into your home or to feel so much guilt.

When they do pass, know they are with you in spirit and there may be times you see a flash out of the corner of your eye like a shadow, or you hear or smell them or you just know they're there. When you sense them in some way, they are with you.

DEHYDRATION

My Thoughts

There are an enormous number of dogs and cats I see who are dehydrated. If you notice cats drinking excessively this may be worth a Vet visit to ensure they don't have any urinary tract or kidney problems or other health concerns.

Considerations

- Cats receive their moisture from their food mostly. If they are eating mostly or only dried food (kibble), they are not being hydrated.
- Cats' tongues are not designed to successfully bring water into their mouth. Did you know, it takes around 2400 dips of the tongue for the cat to take in one quarter cup of water? It must come from their food.
- Dogs eating kibble/dried food and not drinking enough, particularly during winter are not being hydrated.

Tips and Suggestions

- Raw Feeding will provide moisture. *See Resources for further information.*
- If your dog doesn't drink much, drop a small amount of beef broth into their water to entice them to drink.
- Remove kibble/dried food from their diet. *See Resources for further information.*
- Ensure there is always access to water.
- Keep water bowls full, clean and fresh.

- It might not appeal to your senses, but keep toilet lids open, access open to showers and sinks for your cats. If they are searching for water, they may need a Vet visit. Sidenote: do not use toilet cistern cleaners/fresheners such as Blue Loo.

DEPRESSION & SADNESS

My Thoughts

Animals have emotional and mental health issues as we do. While those big sad dog eyes may not indicate they are sad, it is important to observe and get to know their mood and temperament so you have a benchmark.

Possible Reasons

- Boredom—cats are often bored, particularly indoor cats.
- Mistreatment.
- Rejection and abandonment.
- Nutrition.
- Being ignored and/or left alone.
- Grief.
- Being yelled at.

Tips and Suggestions

- Be present with your animals. This means, pat them, speak with them, play with them and be fully engaged. Put your phone down, your emails to the side and give them your full and undivided attention.
- Many animals need friends and companions (including horses who I often see alone and depressed).
- Play with your cats every day, they need mental and physical stimulation. Fish-on-a-string toys work well.
- Ensure their food is species specific *(*See Resources)*.
- Remove kibble and dried food from your cat or dog's diet.

- Don't separate animals that are friends unless there is no other option. If there is no other option, speak to them and tell them where they're going and why.
- If you are going away on holiday, don't leave your dog or cat a bowl full of kibble and close the door. Employ a pet sitter that can feed them adequately, clean their litter trays, give them fresh filtered water and company.

ELDERLY ANIMALS

My Thoughts

It's a sad truth that our animals age and as they come into their senior years they will need more help from you. When I have taken my old dogs out walking, I pick points along the way to ask them if they want to go home or keep walking. Using telepathy (impressing images, words, feelings into their mind) I would ask, "If you want to go home now, turn around and walk towards home or if you want to keep going, walk straight ahead. Remember, you have to go back the same distance you came out." I might wait a minute before they would decide, but they would always show me what they wanted to do. They know how their body feels better than anyone, so give them the choice to decide.

I communicate with many dogs that have dementia type diseases like Sundowner Syndrome. They are still able to communicate with clarity through an Animal Communicator. What you see may be stressful, but it is often not how they feel. I would highly recommend checking in with them, particularly as their health begins to decline.

Tips and Suggestions

- Pay attention to your flooring and how your pets are slipping and sliding on them. This can cause injury and discomfort. Trim their nails and the hairs between their pads so the feet can get traction on the floor. You can also purchase Toe Grips that adhere to your dog's toenails that prevent slipping.
- For older animals, reduce the length of their walks.

- If you run with your dog, pay close attention to them and be smart with whether they should still be running and how far is far enough.
- Regular Chiropractic, Osteopathic, Bodywork maintenance.
- Use telepathy to ask them how far they want to or are able to walk.
- If you have a pet with dementia or Sundowners Syndrome their Soul is still very clear with what it needs from you. Enlist an Animal Communicator to be the connection between you so you can understand how they're feeling and what they need. *For information on how to work with me, see Find Rommie Buhler Online.*
- Older dogs can become more fearful of loud sounds as they age. Possible tools to work with fear of noises:
  - Emotional Freedom Technique (EFT) *(*See Resources).*
  - Specifically composed music *(*See Resources).*
  - Tellington T. Touch *(*See Resources).*
  - Shamanic Healing.
  - Energy Healing.
  - Flower Essences.
  - Correct Nutrition.
  - Acupuncture/Acupressure.
  - Crystals.
  - CBD Oil for animals.
  - Hemp Chews.
  - Chakra Balancing (including the 8th Brachial "Bonding" Chakra).
  - Body wraps.

EXCESSIVE BARKING

My Thoughts

Barking is a difficult one to manage. Dogs bark for various reasons, such as:
- Boredom.
- Alerting you to someone being on your property.
- Anxiety and fear.
- Protecting their people.

Tips and Suggestions
- Enlist a specialist dog trainer and/or behaviourist.
- Using the correct language when speaking to them. (*See Talking to Animals for Better Behaviour).
- Consistency, persistence, commitment and ensuring everyone in the house is on the same page when changing these behaviours.

FEEDING

My Thoughts

It is critical we feed our animals a nutritionally sound diet for their physical and psychological health. Unless they are living wild, they cannot feed themselves; they are 100% reliant on you for their health. Kibble has zero nutritional value and should never be a consideration. It is a food of convenience that is causing major disease, creating behavioural and emotional problems and/or ultimately killing our pets. If you want your animals to live well, feed them well. Cats and dogs should be fed an appropriate and balanced diet. It may take some trial and error to work out exactly what to feed your animals, but persist, it is one of the most valuable things you will ever do for them. Not to mention the reduced stress for you as their caretaker and fewer Vet visits.

I am also aware that many people forget to feed their animals or don't see their hunger and needs as important (or as essential as their own). You would never not feed yourself, so don't forget your animals.

Tips and Suggestions

- Remove kibble from their diet— it is killing them.
- Raw food diets for cats and dogs are highly nutritious (*See Resources).
- If you commonly forget to feed your pet, set an alarm to remind you.
- Don't disregard them when they're telling you they are hungry and it's time for them to be fed. If they are eating foods that have little or no nutritional value, their body is probably starving for nutrition.

- If you have your children feeding your animals, ensure they are doing what they say.
- Don't overfeed your animals. Being overweight causes stress on the body and increases the possibility of major disease.
- Make yourself familiar with what supplements may be required by your animal. Nearly all dogs and cats I see have digestive disorders. As with humans, gut health is an important consideration for animals.
- Feeding appropriate 'cooling' or 'heating' foods for their body/time of year, etc. A Holistic Vet that specializes in Traditional Chinese Veterinary Medicine can assist.
- Make yourself familiar with your local Animal Nutritionists, Animal Naturopaths and Traditional Chinese Veterinary Medical practitioners. Learn from these people that have the knowledge and experience.

GROOMING AND BRUSHING

Grooming

I have had dogs that have shown me what it feels like when they have been excessively groomed; that is taking off their full coat. This wasn't done because there was uncomfortable matting and knots, but because their people thought it must be hot for them under all that fur in the middle of summer. This is a part of their heating and cooling mechanism and no amount of panting, sitting in cool dirt or the shade can help them regulate their temperature.

- Brush them regularly to remove the undercoat and reduce the knotting and matting.
- Don't let your idea of what's too hot determine what you do with your pet's coat length.

Brushing

Some animals love it, some loathe it, but why should we do it:

- It keeps their coat healthy and distributes the oils evenly.
- In my experience it greatly reduces the number of hairballs your cats cough up and that's a win for me!
- It can help reduce the knotting and matting that can be painful for your animals as it pulls on the skin.
- It removes the undercoat which can help with heat regulation.
- It reduces the amount of hair floating around your house (another win!).
- If you have an animal that loves brushing, this feels like the best scratch they've ever had.
- Don't overbrush them, particularly cats or animals with fine hair, you may pull out so much hair you draw blood so ensure you are paying attention while you are brushing.

HOLIDAYING WITHOUT YOUR PETS

My Thoughts

Animals understand us and it is important you communicate with them when you are planning a holiday or business trip away. This can help reduce anxiety when they're at a boarding facility or with a house sitter. Leaving Flower Essences for Anxiety with your house sitter or boarding facility can greatly help if your animal is prone to separation anxiety.

Tips and Suggestions
- As you would tell the people in your life, let your animals know as soon as you are aware that you will be going away. This may help reduce their anxiety while you are gone.
  - Tell them where you are going and how long you will be away.
  - They may not have clocks and calendars on tap, but they do understand the passing of time. If you were going to do the shopping for two hours you would use two hours, but when you are away for days/nights, you need to speak in terms of a full day. I have learned that they understand "dark nights" equating to a full day. For example, you might say, "I'm going camping and I'll be back in 6 dark nights".
- Tell them, but also show them in images (imagine you're impressing the image from your mind to theirs) who is going to be looking after them.
- While you are away, talk to them often even if you can't hear their answers and send them the feeling of your love. And while you may feel you don't understand

them, pay attention to any images or thoughts that come to mind, it may well be them talking to you or answering your questions.
- On many occasions, your animals know you need a break and encourage you to take time out.

HORSE BITS

My Thoughts

I have not met a single horse that enjoys wearing a Bit. There are a variety of Bits available and each horse will find one better than the other, but at the end of the day, none of them are comfortable. The best description I have for what this feels like to them is if you can imagine swallowing and gagging on your own tongue. Sounds uncomfortable, doesn't it! If you are competing, it is out of your hands if the rules require them, but I encourage you to find the least aggravating one for your horse. An Animal Communicator that can feel what your animal is feeling can help you with this (*For information on how to work with me, see Find Rommie Buhler Online.)

Outside of competition I would highly recommend adjusting to Bitless for the sake of your horse and their comfort.

HORSES MISBEHAVING

My Thoughts
When horses become difficult and obstreperous, firstly check they are not injured. What I have found is, if a horse enjoys and wants to compete in the discipline they are being trained for and they are happy with their world and they start acting out, they are often responding to pain. Of course, there is lameness, numerous diseases, misunderstanding and confusion, injuries and pain location points that can be a problem—I am coming from the perspective of what I mostly see in my clients—very often I see pain in the lumbar area, nerve impingement, neck pain and/or withers and shoulder pain.

It can be like finding a needle in a haystack, but if your Vet is unable to locate the root of the problem, an Animal Communicator may be able to work with you to ascertain more information that can assist them. Know too that this may not always be a physical pain, but an emotional one.

Tips and Suggestions
- Contact an Animal Communicator or Medical Intuitive to help determine location of pain, root of pain, reasons behind pain or injury, etc (*For information on how to work with me, see Find Rommie Buhler Online.)*

INAPPROPRIATE TOILET HABITS

My Thoughts
Animals are generally very clean and once they have been toilet trained, they should do their 'business' in their designated locations. When a cat is peeing outside their litter tray or a dog is pooing under the bed, they are trying to get a message to their person—this is rarely an act of defiance.

Possible Reasons
- Urinary Tract or other Illness (see Vet).
- Not enough litter trays.
- Litter feels uncomfortable underfoot.
- May not like the size of the tray.
- Litter trays are not clean.
- Not enough litter in the tray.
- They've never used a litter tray previously or are not toilet trained.
- Inhouse fighting.
- Stress and anxiety.

Tips and Suggestions
- Rule of thumb on cat trays is one tray per cat, plus one. Some cats like one pee tray and one poop tray and if you have more than one cat in the house this may mean you need more trays. Play around until you find the right number. When I've spoken to people about this, I am often told, "Too bad, they'll get what they're given, or I don't have the room". This is dismissive and disrespectful to your animal and your reward may be more of the same behaviour.
- Find the litter your cat likes.

- Find the right tray—size, enclosed, open—all cats are different.
- Empty trays when used and wash them out before refilling.
- Toilet training.
- Animal Communication to determine the why. *(*For information on how to work with me, see Find Rommie Buhler Online).*
- Anxiety. *(*See Anxiety)*
- Rule out any illness with your Vet.
- Use words that show them the behaviour you want. *(*See Talking to Animals for Better Behaviour).*

ITCHING, SCRATCHING, LICKING AND CHEWING—DOGS

My Thoughts
I have seen so many dogs that scratch, lick and chew paws, lick noses until they're almost raw and gnaw until lesions form. It is a complex problem and there are many more reasons than I have listed or even know about, but I will share some of the common ones I see.

Possible Reasons
- Food.
  - Highly processed canned foods and kibble.
  - Some things I commonly see that are causing a problem:
    - Carrots, particularly in short haired dogs.
    - Rosemary extract.
    - Spinach.
    - Coconut Oil.
    - Turmeric.
  - Feeding foods that are too 'hot' for an animal that is already hot. *(*See Dr. Judy Morgan's Book, Yin & Yang Nutrition for Dogs in the Resources.)*
  - Feeding foods that are too 'cool' for an animal that is already cold. *(*See Dr. Judy Morgan's in the Resources.)*
- Allergies.
- Anxiety.
- Chemicals *(See the extended list of chemicals)*.
  - We don't need a pretty smelling home; we just need a clean one so find natural alternatives to highly toxic cleaning products.
  - Know when and what is being sprayed in your local parks, nature reserves and neighbouring properties and stay away as required.

- An excess of heat in their body. Your dog will be looking for cool places to be (shaded areas, etc). They may also have a red tongue. *(*See Dr. Judy Morgan in the Resources.).*

Tips and Suggestions
- Removing kibble and highly processed canned food from your cats/dog's diet.
- Raw Food Eating for cats and dogs *(*See Resources).*
- Traditional Chinese Veterinary Medicine can be extremely helpful with determining if your animal has too much heat or cold in their body and what foods can help bring them back into balance.

Both Hair Mineral Analysis Testing and **Bio Compatability Hair Testing** can also be helpful in getting your animal's health back on track. Not all tests are available to all animals, but it is worth checking around to see if you can find someone that does testing on your particular animal. Some do only cats and dogs, some horses and dogs, some anything from sheep to camels to dogs, cats, horses. It is very simple and painless as you are cutting hair off your animal and sending it off to a lab.

HAIR MINERAL ANALYSIS TESTING
When animals are exposed to toxic heavy metals, they can suffer and get sick. Animals are exposed to all sorts of heavy metals in their everyday environment from their food, drinking water, drinking water from areas like ponds, dams, creeks, their containers, insecticides, medication, shampoos, etc.

If your animal has:
- Unusual behaviours like eating dirt or debarking trees
- Flaky skin
- Tooth decay
- A rough coat

this can indicate mineral imbalances that can long term lead to disease and ill health.

A **Hair Mineral Analysis Test** will determine what is missing from your animal's diet, including mineral deficiencies and toxicities. It will also detect levels of heavy metals in their body to ultimately encourage better health, prevent disease, cancers and premature aging.

BIO COMPATIBILITY HAIR TESTING

This is a test that analyses the compatibility of items with your animal. Do you research for the right laboratory as there are places that will test 200 items and there are others that will test more like 600 items.

When your animal has digestive disorders, itchy skin, rashes, allergies, inflammation, arthritis and behavioural problems it is worth investigating this compatibility test for checking compatibility on anything from food, shampoos, medications, bedding, grasses, oils, supplements, cigarette smoke, dustmite, mosquitoes, tennis balls, fleas and much more.

Sidenote: You can often get clues as to where your animal may be unwell in their body by noticing their skin and coat. Make sure you have a baseline to work from so take photos from various angles of your animal now to keep for comparison.

> *If the hair/coat/skin is looking unusual, lack lustre, growing in an odd pattern or direction there may be something deeper going on in that particular part of their body. For example, I had a cat with kidney cancer and the hair across the kidneys sat in a permanent hair part. It was one of the few things I noticed that sent me to the vet for tests and stayed that way until he passed.*

MIRRORING BEHAVIOUR

My Thoughts
Animals often mirror our behaviour, whether it's a physical problem, an emotion, our energy or even a personality trait. Pay attention to the hyper dog that jumps all over everyone and notice if that is your behaviour, or the person who is feeling highly stressed and anxious that is reflecting back in their dog, or the cat that is overeating and putting on weight to show you that you need to watch your diet. Notice that back injury in your animal that reflects your back injury (or the emotions of that injury) you're not dealing with.

I have seen in many sessions with clients that our animals choose us before they come to the planet and while they have their own journey in life, they are also here to help us learn and grow and mirroring is one way they do this. All we need to do is pay attention to their wisdom so we can journey inward and find that place of peace.

Tips and Suggestions
Sometimes it's difficult to see how we're behaving or what's going on with us. Try writing down three words to describe your animal's personality and then write three words to describe your own. Write down three words to describe your energy and emotions and do the same for your animal. Do you see any correlation? If you have trouble with this, ask someone that knows you well to do it for you.

MISSING & STOLEN ANIMALS

MISSING ANIMALS

Animals go missing all day, every day. They are stolen, get themselves lost or they leave of their own accord. Never assume that this won't happen to you. Stay vigilant and be prepared. Make yourself familiar with all avenues you can follow to find your missing animals including Intuitive Investigators, Pet Detectives, Missing Animal Investigators, Animal Communicators. *(*For information on how to work with me, see Find Rommie Buhler Online)*

A study[1] completed in 2018 suggests 75% of cats were found within a 500 metre (0.3 miles) radius of their point of escape. A preliminary, non-scientific study by the Missing Pet Partnership in 2011 determined 84% of escaped *outdoor* cats were found within a 5-house radius of their home and 92% *indoor* only cats were found within a 5-house radius of their home.

Let me tell you, cats get into everything from washing machines to pool filter enclosures, to ceiling spaces to stormwater drains to bird boxes to garden sheds, under decks, garages, neighbours' boats and so many other nooks and crannies and you need to be prepared to get down and dirty and search.

What I have found is people are happy to place flyers in the mailboxes of their neighbours or even knock on their door, but they are not getting into their yards and looking into all possibilities. Your neighbours are not going to look for your pets like you are. Ask them if you can search their yards.

Tips and Suggestions

- Have all the necessary items in place that you could pull out at a moment's notice.
  - **Photos.** A photo of your animal that is in full view, standing with eyes open and tail showing.
  - Take photos (and a video can be helpful) of any markings that are significant, a broken/bent/quirky tail, scars, limps, etc. Keep this at the ready for posters, flyers and Facebook pages.
  - **Microchip Number.** Are your animals chipped? It's a good idea to do that. Do you have their number handy? Get it out. If you have changed address, make sure you have updated those details on the database.
  - **Proof of Identity.** All laws are different across countries, but make sure you have proof that you own your animal. If someone is caring for your animal while they're trying to find you, you can show they belong to you. If they have been stolen, you will want this information in your toolbox.
- Make sure your animals are secure within your vehicle in the event a door is opened. You don't want them escaping into traffic or getting lost in an unfamiliar area.
- Be open to the idea that your animal is not happy with circumstances in their home and they have left of their own accord. This is very common when a new partner joins the household that they are not happy about.
- Animals will leave (or pass) if their "job here on earth or with that particular person is done". There are few people I speak with that like to entertain this idea, but it is worth keeping in mind as it does happen more often than you may like to think.

- Contact an Intuitive Investigator to help you with your search. *(*For information on how to work with me, see Find Rommie Buhler Online)*

STOLEN DOGS

Dog theft is big business. Thieves are getting bolder and taking pets in broad daylight right in front of your face. Make sure you are aware of what's going on around you. Dogs are going out the door like hotcakes so stay vigilant.

Tips and Suggestions
- Don't leave them unmonitored in vehicles.
- Don't tie them up unmonitored at shopping centres.
- Keep your yard gate deadlocked.
- Make sure your dogs aren't visible from the front of your house.
- Fix up any holes in fences.
- Pay attention to strange people and/or cars in your area that may be scoping and watching your house, etc.

Search Methods Used to Locate Missing Cats and Locations Where Missing Cats Are Found Liyan Huang,1 Marcia Coradini,1, Jacquie Rand,1,2 John Morton,3 Kat Albrecht,4 Brigid Wasson,4 and Danielle Robertson4. PMID: 29301322. 2 January 2018.

NAIL TRIMMING

My Thoughts
Cats and dogs need their nails trimmed regularly if they're not spending time outside on a variety of ground surfaces that naturally keep them shortened. There is a right and wrong way to trim nails so ask your Vet if you need guidance.

Also, if your dog is walking on slippery surfaces (e.g., polished floorboards or tiles), make sure you are cutting the hair between their toe pads to help with traction and to avoid injury. Toe Grips are also available that adhere to each individual nail to stop slipping.

When nails are too long:
- It can put undue pressure on different parts of the body making it difficult to walk or run and cause pain and injury.
- The force goes back into the nail bed, creating pain.
- There is less traction.
- They can tear and split, causing pain.
- They can curl and grow back into their pad which is painful.
- They are more susceptible to injury.

NAMING ANIMALS

My Thoughts
Naming an animal is an important consideration. **It is not a laughing matter to them so name them with an appropriate intention.**

Many animals do not like their names either because it doesn't suit them or because their person thought it was funny and were making a joke of them. The same way we like or don't like our names, our animals feel the same. Think about the personality of your animal or what energy you're trying to help them evoke and name them with thought and consideration. Timid animals will often like names that symbolise bravery and courage.

PAIN

My Thoughts

Animals will not show pain unless it is extreme, for fear of being attacked or killed. This is innate wiring that is to help keep them safe and alive. You need to know this, because many of your animals will be in pain and you won't know about it. Make yourself familiar with your pet so you have a benchmark to know what's changed.

What to Look for
- Cats
  - Over grooming a particular area.
  - Sleeping more.
  - Hiding.
  - Their movements appear stiff. While cats may look sure on their feet, they can mistime and fall and injure themselves.
  - Biting or hissing when touched.
  - Peeing outside litter tray (usually they are trying to get a message to you).
  - Mood changes.
- Dogs
  - Change in breathing—excessive panting, shallow breathing.
  - Biting, aggression, temperament change.
  - Sleeping more.
  - Energy levels changing.
  - Can't seem to get comfortable.
  - Challenged getting up and down, in or out of vehicles, etc.
  - Limping or holding a leg up is usually quite obvious.
  - Trembling.

- Horses
  - Biting an area of their body or if they can't reach, staring at it.
  - Changes in head posture; the way they carry their head.
  - Losing weight and/or changes in feeding and appetite.
  - Injury, unusual posture and/or swelling, shifting weight from one leg to another.
  - Grinding teeth, excessive drooling.
  - Lameness, abnormal gait.
  - Change in coat.
  - Tail not moving freely and/or tucked.
  - Sweating out of the ordinary.
  - Laying down more often than normal.
  - Muscle tremors.
  - Unusual behaviours—acting stubborn, not wanting to move, etc.
  - Reactions to things like grooming or saddle/bit/bridle.
  - Temperament changes.
  - Squinting or worried eyes.

Tips and Suggestions
- There are many ways of treating pain, and it is always worth consulting with your Vet first. Try everything you can before an invasive surgery. Some options I have seen helpful (making sure you are working with animal specific practitioners that know and understand the anatomy of your animal):
  - Chiropractic
  - Osteopathy
  - Acupuncture

- Laser Therapy
  - Tellington T. Touch
  - Emotional Freedom Technique (EFT)
  - Equine Mechanic
  - Bowen Therapist
  - Specialist Dentist
  - Animal Nutritionist
  - Animal Naturopath
  - Holistic Veterinarian

- Learn more about silent pain in animals and what to look for. (*See Dr Edward Bassingthwaighte in the Resources.)

PAW PAD BURNS | HEAT & COLD

HEAT BURNS

An air temperature of 25°C | 77°F, which may feel quite pleasant on your person, can turn asphalt into a burning hot 52°C | 125°F paw pad burner. Did you know, it takes 60 seconds for a pad to burn in this heat. It's quick and incredibly painful.

If you can't rest the back of your hand on a hot surface for five seconds, it is too hot for your dog. It is not only asphalt, but all surfaces such as brick, metal, sand and artificial grass can heat up very quickly. Burnt pads can be easily prevented by avoiding extreme heat and checking surface temperatures before you take your dog out walking, on adventure or visiting your local market (I see dogs at markets trying to pull their owners to the shade all the time so my suggestion is leave them at home when it's hot).

If your dog has burnt their paw pads you may recognise this by certain behaviours like:

- Limping.
- Licking their paws.
- Being vocal when using the burnt foot.
- Holding their paw up away from the ground.
- More obviously they will be bleeding, ulcerated and red.

AIR TEMPERATURE	ASHPALT TEMPERATURE
25°C	77°F	52°C	125°F
35°C	95°F	65°C	149°F

ICE BURNS

Ice burn, frostbite and hypothermia can be a huge problem for animals when the temperature plummets. If it is too cold for you, it is too cold for your pet.

Tips and Suggestions.
- Wash and dry your pets' feet in warm water after they've been outside. Salt and chemicals used on roads can irritate and burn pads.
- Antifreeze is extremely poisonous and can be a big problem if you are spraying your frozen windows or it leaks from your radiator.
  - Clean up any spills so your animals don't walk through these leaks and lick their paws.
  - Ensure antifreeze is locked away.
- When you go out, keep your animals inside and keep the heating on in your house. Houses can be cold when unheated.
- Note that short nosed dogs can suffer from breathing conditions and heat stroke in freezing conditions when going from the freezing cold to inside a warm house. Pay attention to their behaviour.
- Avoid ice and slippery surfaces to avoid injury, particularly for animals with joint problems, arthritis, etc.
- Make sure your dog is secured inside your vehicle and you help them out when you are parked to avoid slipping injuries like strains and tears with them jumping out of your car.
- Consider purchasing wax for pad protection (something Musher's use that is very effective).
- Animals can easily get lost in blizzard conditions, ensure they are collared and microchipped.

- Consider jumpers and boots for your dogs.
- Cats have a habit of finding their way to heated vehicles so before you drive off check under your car, the wheel hubs and under the bonnet to make sure they're not curled up somewhere cosy.

POO ABNORMALITIES IN CATS AND DOGS

Tips and Suggestions

You may not be that excited to analyse your cat or dog's poo, but it is worth making yourself familiar with what can highlight problems that need to be addressed. There are four areas of interest that you need to be aware of—these are commonly referred to as the Four Cs.

1. **Consistency**
    a. A normal poo is a lot like Goldilocks laying down to sleep…the first bed is too hard, the second too soft and the third was just right! It should be not too hard, not too mushy, but firm yet pliable.
    b. Pay attention to greasy, watery, mushy, soft, chalky, tarry, hard poos. If in doubt, consult with your Vet.
2. **Coating**
    a. There should not be a coating.
    b. Excess mucous is worthy of a consult with your Vet.
3. **Colour**
    a. A healthy poo is a chocolate brown. Having said that, there are many variables to what is "normal" including breed, diet, hydration, colourings used in foods, etc. Make yourself familiar with what is your animal's version of healthy brown. I'd suggest taking a photo (with no filters) and keeping this handy to compare.
    b. See more on colour below.

4. **Contents**
    a. You should not see any unusual substances in the poo.

As I always say, "If in doubt, take your pet to the Vet". But before you do, bag a poo and take it with you for further analysis.

COLOURS
- **BROWN**
    - This is the normal poo. Chocolate brown and its variations are dependent on breed, diet, etc. as mentioned above.
- **BLACK OR VERY DARK**
    - Sticky, tar-like, very dark in colour.
    - This may indicate partially digested blood from ulcerations in the upper gastrointestinal tract.
    - Consult with your Vet.
- **BRIGHT RED OR RED STREAKS**
    - This may indicate undigested blood lower down in the gastrointestinal tract.
    - May be inflammation of the colon, rectal injury, or anal gland infection.
    - Consult with your Vet.
- **PINK/PURPLE**
    - Described as Raspberry Jam Poo because of the blood and mucous that makes it look like jam. I know, I know, that's not a good visual!
    - This is very serious. Consult with your Vet.
- **GREY AND GREASY**
    - Digestive system may be struggling to break down fats.

- ○ Possibly relates to eating too much fatty food or an issue with the pancreas' digestion of fats.
- ○ If in doubt, consult with your Vet.
- **GREEN**
  - ○ May be eating large amounts of grass.
  - ○ Possible sign of poisons, e.g. rat bait or parasites.
  - ○ If in doubt, consult with your Vet.
- **ORANGE**
  - ○ When the food moves through the digestive system too quickly for the bile to make it look "normal".
  - ○ If in doubt, consult with your Vet.
- **YELLOW**
  - ○ Often a sign of a food intolerance.
  - ○ Make a note of what they're eating and work through a process of elimination.
  - ○ If there have been no food changes and they haven't eaten anything while out and about, consult with your Vet for further investigation.
- **WHITE WITH SPECKLES**
  - ○ Specks look like white rice grains.
  - ○ May be worms.
  - ○ Consult with your Vet for further advice and treatment.
- **WHITE AND CHALKY**
  - ○ May be too much calcium.
  - ○ A high mineral diet or too many bones can chalk the poo.
  - ○ Reduce amount of bone and minerals being fed.
  - ○ If unsure or in doubt, consult with your Vet.

PURCHASING ANIMALS

Tips and Suggestions.
- **Competition Animals**
  - If you are purchasing a **competition animal**, you will be looking for certain attributes, some you see or will know about, some you don't. Animal Communication is a useful option to consider at the pre-purchase stage so you can determine whether they will be what you need them to be, you will know if they want to train and compete for that discipline you are buying them for, you will get a heads up on any potential health issues that may come up or need attention.
  - The last thing an animal wants is to be rehomed because they are not what you wanted or expected.
  - Contact an Animal Communicator for a pre-purchase report. (*For information on how to work with me, see Find Rommie Buhler Online)*

Buying Large Animals
  - Nutrition plays such a vital role in your animal's health and welfare that it is an absolute must to consider whether you can afford to feed the **large dog/s** (or any large animal) you want to bring into your home. It is irresponsible to want a large dog as your mate and only be able to afford a kibble with empty nutrition and preservative filled canned food. It is not only unfair to set them on a course of feeling continually unwell and being able to do nothing about it, but it is also setting them up for

> major disease (that will cost a lot of money and heartache at the Vet). Consider an animal you can afford to feed nutritionally well and if that's a Chihuahua and not a Rottweiler then that is what it should be.

SADDLE FIT

My Thoughts

It is worth remembering that as the seasons come and go and your horse's physique changes accordingly, a once well fitted saddle may no longer suit. I see many saddles that don't fit and cause withers and shoulder pain and discomfort.

Tips and Suggestions

- Have your saddle fitted by a reputable professional.
- Change or alter accordingly with body shape changes.
- If you are borrowing a saddle from another horse, ensure the fit is correct.

STATIC SHOCK

My Thoughts

When the nervous system is under duress, it can make animals feel anything from boiling hot and uncomfortable, to this sensation of constant electric shocks running through their entire body and inside their skull. There is static everywhere and it can cause great discomfort, change in behaviour, mood, physical energy and overall health.

Considerations

- Static from:
  - Synthetic blankets on horses.
  - Synthetic bedding for some of our household animals like cats, dogs and rabbits.
  - Synthetic animal jackets and clothing.
  - Various carpets and floorings.

Tips and Suggestions

- Change blankets, bedding, jackets, clothing, etc to natural fibres.
- Humidifiers to add moisture to air.
- Light spray mist on fur.
- Wooden or metal brushes (not plastic).

SUNBURN

My Thoughts

Animals get sunburned and it can be very painful. Stay aware and pay attention to what's going on around them. This is a much bigger problem than you may think.

- Keep them in the shade.
- Apply natural animal only sunscreen on them.
- Re-consider how much hair you cut off in summer.
- Limit their time in the sun.

TALKING TO ANIMALS FOR BETTER BEHAVIOUR

My Thoughts

The words we use when speaking with our animals are important. Animals are telepathic, which means they are reading the images you have placed there showing them you're okay with them barking, pooping inside the house, pulling up at a jump, etc. We effectively are showing our animals through images how we DON'T want them to behave.

We are wired to say *No, Don't, Stop,* and *Can't* and all those negative words and the problem with this is the images in our mind don't represent stopping or changing that behaviour and that's what our animals are viewing. We need to use the words that create the images of the behaviour we DO want. For example, your dog jumps up on everyone that walks through the door, including that friend with her perfectly pressed white pants. You know she's coming for a visit and you know Rusty's going to jump because he always does. You play this video over in your mind as you wait for the doorbell to ring. It rings and Rusty, who has just run back inside from that mud patch out back jumps all over your friend (who is now offering you her drycleaning bill) and you yell, "Noooo Rusty, stop. Don't jump. You have nervously been rolling that video screen through your mind of exactly what's going to happen, before and during this 'hello exchange' and guess what.... it plays out perfectly!

Better wording to use might be something like, *Put your feet on the floor* or *All four paws on the floor*. It doesn't need to be technical; it just needs to create an image of the behaviour you want from them.

This goes with training and competing animals. When you have a horse that isn't doing what you ask of them in eventing or show jumping, etc, notice what is going on in your mind before the event and during the event. Change the video, see your horse gliding over those jumps with freedom and ease, see your horse jump without hesitation from a starting barrier before their race. Take them around the course and show them with images how you're going to work together and what you want from them.

Tips and Suggestions
Make a list of the problem behaviours and write next to it what words you are currently using to change that behaviour. Pay attention to what images those words may be creating. Then write down your new wording and then practise it until it becomes a habit. While you're driving, wandering through the supermarket, sitting outside staring at the wilderness, repeat it over and over again until they are the only words you use. If you have others in your house, you all need to be speaking the same language so make sure you're all onto it. An example below to get started.

When you are calm and giving your animals direction with the right images (language), they will know what to do.

Animals Speak

CHANGING THE WAY YOU SPEAK WITH YOUR ANIMALS FOR BETTER BEHAVIOUR

PROBLEM EXAMPLES	WORDS YOU CURRENTLY USE	NEW LANGUAGE FOR BETTER BEHAVIOUR
Barking Dogs [dogs]	Stop Barking. No Barking. Don't Bark.	Be Quiet. Close Your Mouth. Ssssshhhh.
Pooing inside [any animal]	Don't poo inside. Stop pooing inside the house.	Poo outside please. Go to the toilet outside.
Pulling up at jumps. [horses]	No, don't stop here. Don't stop at that jump.	Let's glide over this jump. Free flow over this jump.
Wanting to go outside. [any animal]	No, you can't go outside. Stop it, you can't go out.	We are inside now. We are staying inside now. It's inside time now.

A few examples that you can adapt to suit the problem you are experiencing with your animals.

VOMITING

My Thoughts

I recommend taking a photo of the vomit before you clean it up to help your Vet understand what may be wrong with your animal.

In my own experience with animals, I have had to consult with our Vet when:

- Vomit is pink or bloody or speckled.
- Vomit is frothy.
- Vomiting is continual (or frequent).
- Vomit is yellow and thick.
- Vomiting is nothing but dry retching.
- If in any doubt, see your Vet.

Chemicals can be fatal to your animals. Always remember many animals have their noses close to the ground sniffing and sometimes licking and chewing poisons at ground level (or rolling in it and grooming themselves).

Possible Reasons
- Internal Issues.
- Food.
- Chemicals and Toxins *(*See full list under Chemicals)*.
    - New Carpets and Flooring.
    - Weed Killer sprayed at your home or neighbourhood.
    - Painting internally or externally.
    - Cleaning products.
    - Certain plants.
    - Aflatoxin in soil.

- - Many aromatherapy oils are toxic to animals.
  - Plug-in air fresheners.
  - Plug-in calming devices.
- Anxiety (*See Anxiety).
- A thousand other reasons.

Tips and Suggestions
- If in doubt, don't wait, consult your Vet.
- Keep animals away from house renovations. At certain times you may need to have them cared for away from home base.
- Use natural and non-toxic cleaning products inside and outside the house.
- Remove toxic weed killing sprays, gardening products, snail pellets, rat baits, etc.
- Keep them away from toxic soil.
- Removing kibble and highly processed canned food from your cats/dog's diet.
- Raw Food Eating for cats and dogs. (*See Resources).

WHISKER STRESS IN CATS & DOGS

My Thoughts

I had a cat who would eat the middle of his food or throw food out of his bowl onto the floor to eat. He would stalk around the bowl quite agitated. I asked him one day why he did this and he told me it hurt his whiskers. A cat's whiskers help them navigate their environment and they are extremely sensitive and a high edged bowl does not feel good to them.

For a dog, having their heads down digging holes or running through bushes doesn't bother them. What can be a problem is constant rubbing so if you have a muzzle that doesn't fit well, this can be very uncomfortable.

Whisker stress can create great mental and physical health disorders, never cut or remove whiskers from your animal.

Tips and Suggestions
- Put their food on a flat plate where their head doesn't go into the bowl and their whiskers touch the sides.
- Fill water bowls right to the top.
- Make sure you have a well fitted muzzle.
- Kids (or adults) over patting or rubbing a dog's face is very unpleasant.

RESOURCES

Below is a list of people I follow and recommend.

ANIMAL BEHAVIOUR AND TRAINING

- Dr. Ian Dunbar - https://www.dunbaracademy.com/
- Cesar Millan - https://www.cesarsway.com/
- Sarah Hodgson - https://www.sarahsayspets.com/

ANIMAL NUTRITION

- Dr. Ian Billinghurst - https://drianbillinghurst.com/
  - Book: *Give Your Dog a Bone*
  - The BARF Diet
- Dr. Nick Thompson - https://holisticvet.co.uk/
- Dr. Karen Becker - https://drkarenbecker.com/
  - Book: *Real Food for Healthy Dogs and Cats*
- Raw Pet Medics - https://rawpetmedics.com/
- Dr. Judy Morgan - https://drjudymorgan.com/
  - Book: *Yin & Yang Nutrition for Dogs: Maximizing Health With Whole Foods, Not Drugs*
- DeDe Murcer Moffett - https://rawdogfoodandco.com/why-raw-dog-food/

SOUND BEHAVIOURIST FOR ANIMALS

- Janet Marlow, Pet Acoustics - https://www.petacoustics.com/

UNDERSTANDING SILENT PAIN IN ANIMALS

- Dr. Edward Bassingthwaite - https://thehealingvet.com/

HOW BEST TO TALK TO YOUR ANIMALS

- Terri Steuben is the master of this and I highly recommend her book: Secrets of a Pet Whisperer.

PET LOSS & GRIEF SPECIALIST

- Nancy Gordon - https://nancygordonglobal.com/

ANXIETY

- Dr. Janet Roark - https://essentialoilvet.com/
- Dr. Jean Hofve - https://littlebigcat.com/
- Gary Craig - Emotional Freedom Technique (EFT) https://emofree.com/animals/general-animals/pets-ideas-article.html
- Dr. Bradley Nelson - Emotion Code - https://drbradleynelson.com/learn-to-release-your-pets-trapped-emotions/
- Linda Tellington-Jones - Tellington T. Touch - https://ttouch.com/
- Adele Leas - Jin Shin Jyutsu - https://jsjforyouranimal.com/

HORSE TRAINER

Carlos Tabernaberri - https://whisperingacres.com/

ACKNOWLEDGMENTS

The idea of this book started in October 2021 while lazing on a warm sandy Hamilton Island beach in Queensland. At the time I was filled with enthusiasm as I discussed different angles with my husband and set out right away with pen and notebook. Two stories in, creativity and eagerness dried up and that notebook was parked incomplete into a corner cupboard.

It was 12 months later, feeling somewhat stale with the year when I received a message from my great friend Deena sharing a seven-day book writing retreat event that was coming up. I hesitated for at least 17 seconds before signing up to what was to be the push I needed to finish this first of hopefully many books. So, to Deena, I thank you for not only being my messenger, but for your endless list of ideas and encouragement to keep going.

To Dave Thompson, Davina and all at Inspirational Book Writers for absolutely everything you have done to help get this completed and up in lights. Hands down, this would not have happened without you.

To Jason, the most patient husband you could possibly ask for. This would not have been possible without your belief in me, propping me up every time "that stupid book no-one's going to read" was going back in the corner and your ability to think outside the square and see through my fog when I'd run out of ideas.

To my greatest fans, Mum and Dad, I wouldn't have been able to write anything if you didn't have me in the first place, but for your continual interest and fascination in what I'm doing, excitement, encouragement, pride and support I thank you from the pits of my guts.

To my brother Kim who is always loaded with practical ideas and advice, best on ground sister-in-law Karen who understands me and who can explain to the rest of the family what it is I do and to my awesome nephews Travis and Harrison—you all make my life richer.

To my greatest friend and book swapping cohort Lily Edwards, if you weren't in my life I don't know this book would ever have passed the thought stage. Thank you for your honesty, encouragement and enthusiasm with everything I do.

My inner circle supporters Cricket and Baby Yoda, thank you for reading my stories and giving me the confidence to do something with them and for your constant encouragement. It is a privilege to have you in my life.

To Morgan Lewis, photographer extraordinaire, thank you for your patience and exceptional captures for this book.

To every one of my clients, I thank you for your trust in me and your continued support.

And last, but who really is first, to every single wild or domesticated animal I have spoken to, healed, helped find and to all the ones that haven't crossed my path yet, I thank you for directing your people to me and for your ongoing teachings and refinement of my craft. I take the job of being your voice seriously and I hope I am doing you justice.

FIND ROMMIE BUHLER ONLINE

The Holistic Animal Health Coach

EMAIL ROMMIE: hello@rommiebuhler.com

Website: www.rommiebuhler.com
Facebook: https://www.facebook.com/theholisticanimalhealthcoach
YouTube: https://www.youtube.com/@theholisticanimalhealthcoach
Instagram: https://www.instagram.com/theholisticanimalhealthcoach/
LinkedIn: https://www.linkedin.com/in/the-holistic-animal-health-coach/
TikTok: https://www.tiktok.com/@rommiebuhler

Medium.com: https://medium.com/@rommiebuhler
Podcast Guest: https://podcastguests.com/expert/rommiebuhler/

the ANIMALS' TELEVISION show

EMAIL ROMMIE: rommie@theanimalstelevisionshow.com

Website: www.theanimalstelevisionshow.com
Facebook: https://www.facebook.com/theanimalstelevisionshow

Instagram: https://www.instagram.com/theanimalstelevisionshow/
YouTube: https://www.youtube.com/@theanimalstelevisionshow
Linkedin: https://www.linkedin.com/in/the-holistic-animal-health-coach/

Online Animal Communication Training Course
https://courses.rommiebuhler.com/courses/animal-communication-for-beginners

ONLINE ANIMAL COMMUNICATION TRAINING

Begin the journey to Loving Your Pets Well!

Communicating with animals has the power to transform your relationship with your animal family like nothing else can.

When we can be in conversation with our animals and know what they need and understand how they feel we have the opportunity to change their lives. As we begin to truly understand them and feel their essence, the depth of love and connection we experience is so profound your heart will feel like it's going to explode.

IN THIS ONLINE, SELF-PACED BEGINNER-LEVEL ANIMAL COMMUNICATION COURSE, YOU WILL:

Discover your inner Animal Communicator.

- Learn Rommie's 6 Steps to effectively connect and communicate with animals.
- Understand the fundamentals of telepathy and develop your intuitive senses.
- Learn ways to quiet your mind to get yourself into the "chat zone".
- Overcome your self-doubt and blocks.
- Receive the support from and practise with your fellow students in a private Facebook group.

Let me tell you:

If you LOVE ANIMALS, there is NOTHING more fulfilling than to have a conversation with them!

There are NO pre-requisites to sign up for this course. You have 12 months to get through the course which gives you plenty of time to learn, practice and fully understand all you need to know about animal communication.

This is a foundation level, "let's start with the basics" course designed to help you learn the art of Animal Communication.

THE COURSE INCLUDES:

- Detailed step by step instructions to effectively prepare, connect and communicate with animals.
- A downloadable workbook and blueprint of Rommie's 6 Step Process to supplement your learning and ongoing home practice.
- Access to a community where you can share questions and experiences with other students.

WHO IS THIS COURSE FOR?

- Animal owners to better understand them to deepen their relationship and improve both of their lives.
- Rescue centres | shelters to help understand their past and what they need now.
- Dog trainers | groomers | walkers | therapists to assist with learning to listen and to communicate with clarity.
- Horse trainers | horse owners for their training, behaviour, physical and emotional needs.
- Vets | vet nurses | zookeepers and staff to assist with the understanding of an animal's pain, behaviour, emotions.
- Farmers to help communicate with clarity and learn how to listen to an animal's needs to better understand and care for them.

SIGN UP NOW

https://www.rommiebuhler.com/online-beginner-level-animal-communication-course

HOW HAS THIS BOOK HELPED YOU?

Have you learned or been inspired by a story or information you've read in this book that has helped your animal in some way?
I'd love to hear all about your experience.

Share with Rommie at hello@rommiebuhler.com.

Made in the USA
Monee, IL
09 February 2023